The Rise of the West

The Rise

of the West

Contributing Authors:

Ira Peck, William Johnson, Frances Plotkin

Historical Consultant:

Alvin Bernstein, Ph.D.
Assistant Professor of Ancient History
Cornell University

SCHOLASTIC INC.

New York Toronto London Sydney Auckland

Other titles in this series:
Empires Beyond Europe: Asia, Africa, and the Americas
The Age of Europe
The Modern World

Curriculum Consultants:

William Guardia
San Antonio Independent School District
San Antonio, Texas

Helen Richardson
Fulton County School System
Atlanta, Georgia

Edward L. Praxmarer
Chicago Public School System
Chicago, Illinois

Staff
Project Director: John Nickerson
Editorial Director: Dr. William Goodykoontz
Editor, Social Studies: Stephen M. Lewin
Readability Consultant: Lawrence B. Charry, Ed. D.

Art Direction and Design: Irmgard Lochner
Cover and Text Illustrator: George Ulrich
Production Editor: Nancy Smith
Photo Researcher: Sukey Bullard
Maps by Wilhelmina Reyinga

18 17 16 15 14 13 12 11 10 9   4 5 6 7 8/8
Printed in the U.S.A.

Contents

Art is a guide to the human past—

A guide to how people dressed, and how they worked;

A guide to how they fought, and how they prayed.

In art, civilizations reveal their inner values.

Here the human story begins....

MESOPOTAMIA: Sumer may have been the seedbed of civilization. From its ruins have come many clues to life 4,500 years ago. The panels at far left are found in an 18-inch wooden box. Across the panels march a parade of soldiers (bottom panel) and war prisoners (third panel), going to see the king (top panel, left, wearing sheepskin skirt). Some early kings of Sumer were looked on as gods and portrayed in stone (left). A later king, Hammurabi of Babylon (seated below), drew up one of the world's first codes of law.

EGYPT: "Can you see anything?" "Yes, wonderful things," answered an English archaeologist in 1922. He was looking into the tomb of King Tutankhamen. Among its treasures: a golden throne showing the young king and his wife (below) and a beetle-shaped jewel with a bright blue eye (lower right). Other colorful objects (right) were buried with Egypt's Queen Nefertiti. She was Tutankhamen's mother-in-law.

LET MY PEOPLE GO: *While desert sands nipped the silent Sphinx (above), kingdoms collided and humans were taken into bondage. Egyptians made prisoners pay tribute to the pharaoh (below). Hebrews held captive in Babylon were freed by Persian soldiers (right). The Persian king let the Hebrews return to Jerusalem.*

12

GREECE: The ancient Greeks
excelled as storytellers. Some of
their favorite tales concerned
Athena, guardian of Athens, goddess
of war and wisdom, and protector of
the arts (left). To honor her, the
Greeks built many temples, but none
more beautiful than the Parthenon
on a hill in Athens (top right).
The picture at lower right tells
another Greek story: After the hero
Achilles died, his armor was awarded
to Odysseus, the bravest man still
living. But instead of keeping
the armor, Odysseus (with beard)
handed it to a young son of Achilles.

14

ROME: Roman soldiers belonged to the strongest army
in the world (above). They defended an empire where
wealthy people often spent their leisure hours reading
(right). The fancy dining room at lower right was in
the home of a small-town merchant. Guests could sit by
the sunken fountain and be lulled by summer music.

16

ROME'S FALL: In later years, Rome grew soft. Common people expected entertainment such as that below. Top panel, musicians accompany gladiators. Bottom panel, a whipper forces fighter to unchain a bull and bear. One of the strongest emperors of the period was Constantine (left), who first let Christians worship freely (right). But barbarian tribes kept chipping off pieces of the Roman Empire. Their art is shown in jewels, lower right.

The Adventure Begins

How would you tell the story of your life?

There's one way you *wouldn't* tell it. You wouldn't try to describe what you did every single day. For one thing, you couldn't remember every day. The chances are you can't even remember what you did every day of last week. Most days, you do many of the same things over again. So the days melt together in your memory.

But there are some days of your life which stand out. They're the times when something special happened. Your family moved to another house or apartment. Or you did well in a school sports event. Or you had a great date. Or you broke your leg. These are the days you'd most likely talk about in telling the story of your life.

This book tells the story of humankind. And it does that the same way as you remember your life—picking out the special times. These are the turning points of history. They're the times when things *could* have happened differently. And if they had, we might be living differently now.

Some of the turning points didn't seem important at the time. You know how it is in your own life. A new family moves in across the street. You don't pay much attention. But a few months later, someone in that family has become your best friend. That's how some big changes have happened to humans.

When you tell your own life story, you have to go back only a few years. To tell the story of humans, this book has to go back tens of thousands of years. For that kind of trip, you need some basic equipment.

First of all, you need ways of measuring distances between events. This basic measure of time is the year. But we'll also be talking about the *decade* (10 years) and the *century* (100 years).

Today we're living in the 20th century. To be exact, the 20th century A.D. These letters stand for the Latin words *Anno Domini*—which mean "in the year of the Lord." That's because we count the years from the birth of Jesus Christ. For the time before his birth we use B.C.—"before Christ." And for that time we count the years backward. In "B.C. time," the numbers get bigger as we go farther back in time. Two hundred B.C. came before 100 B.C. Julius Caesar was born in 100 B.C. and died in 44 B.C.

Of course, the people who lived in the years B.C. could not know that they were living in B.C. times. The different people of the ancient world had different ways of counting. The ancient Greeks counted their years from the first Olympic games. The ancient Romans counted from the beginning of Rome. In ancient Egypt and China, each king started a new count when he took over.

We look at the past from our point in time. We talk about *ancient* times—roughly, before 500 A.D. After that, it's *modern* times. But to people living in ancient Greece, their time was modern. And to people living 2,000 years from now, our times may seem very ancient!

Ancient objects often supply clues to the past. Some samples: a game board made of shells (above), a dagger and sheath from a Sumerian cemetery (right), Sumerian writing on a clay tablet (below). Page 20: Scientists explore ancient burial ground at city of Ur.

How do we know what happened in the past? Think of your own past life again. Suppose someone else had to tell your life story — without being able to talk to you. How would they go about it?

Well, they'd look for all kinds of clues. Your birth certificate. The family photo album. Shells you collected on a vacation. An award or a trophy.

There are many similar clues to the human past. The most important are *written records*. Laws. Treaties. Letters. Political speeches. All kinds of clues set down in writing.

But writing was invented only about 6,000 years ago. Before that there were no written records. And for a long time after that, only a few records survived. So we have to look for other clues too.

All kinds of objects remain from long ago. The ruins of buildings. Tools. Weapons. Ornaments. Bones. A lot of these things are found lying under the ground. The ones deeper down were left there earlier than the ones above. This gives us a rough way of telling *when* events happened.

There are other kinds of information we can get from these clues. Suppose we find iron tools in an area where there is no iron ore. We can be pretty sure that the people there must have traded with other people who *did* have iron.

Suppose we find an ancient ruin that shows the marks of fire all around it. Suppose we also find bodies with broken bones and weapons. Can we guess what happened at the ruin?

New discoveries are being made about the past all the time. That makes history new as well as old. It's new because we are always learning something about the past. It's also new because the past has something to say about the present. It shows us how we arrived where we are today. Since we are always learning about the past, our view of it is always changing.

So there is no end to these world adventures. We are still living them at the end of the 20th century A.D.

Marking Time

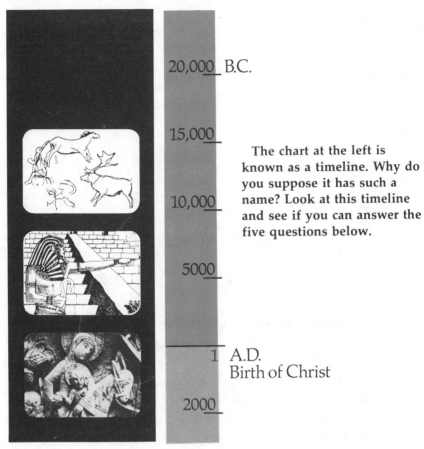

20,000 B.C.

15,000

10,000

5000

1 A.D.
Birth of Christ

2000

The chart at the left is known as a timeline. Why do you suppose it has such a name? Look at this timeline and see if you can answer the five questions below.

- Which date occurred longer ago: 15,000 B.C. or 5000 B.C.?

- Which date is closer to our own time: 2000 A.D. or 5000 A.D.?

- For which period — B.C. or A.D. — is the following statement true? "The larger the number, the longer ago the date occurred."

- How many years are there between 5000 B.C. and 2000 A.D.?

- As of now, which period is longer: the period known as B.C. or the period known as A.D.?

Prologue: Before History

Humans have lived on the earth for about two million years. For most of that time, life was very hard. People had little comfort. Danger was everywhere. People lived in caves or under branches. Most of their waking time was spent searching for food or water.

At some point in time, humans learned to use fire to cook their meat, warm their bodies, and scare off wild animals. They also learned to make simple weapons and tools by chipping pieces off rocks until the rocks had sharp points.

Slowly humans learned to improve their lives. They learned to make better weapons and tools. They discovered better ways of hunting.

But these changes took hundreds of thousands of years. People didn't know their lives were changing. They were too busy finding enough food to stay alive.

Let's go back about 20,000 years. That sounds like a long time ago. It isn't. If you realize that humans have been around for about two million years, 20,000 years isn't so much. Even 20,000 years ago, life was still very tough. But some improvements have come. Can you identify them in the following story?

The Boy stands at the edge of the cliff, a few steps away from the cave. He is still as a tree, listening.

There is a crackling sound. But it is just the fire in front of the cave. It is kept smoldering during the day. The Old Woman sits beside the fire, making sure it does not go out.

There is a tapping sound too, coming from Strong Arm. He twisted his ankle in the hunt yesterday and could not go hunting with the other men today. So he has stayed home, making tools.

Strong Arm sits with a big lump of stone between his knees. He picks up a hard stick. He places one end of the stick on the stone, near the edge. Then he hits the other end with a heavy rock. A sliver of stone breaks away from the lump. The edge of the sliver is sharp. Strong Arm is the best toolmaker in the group.

Suddenly, there is a rustling from the woods in front of the cave. Then voices come drifting up. It is the women coming back from their search for food.

They climb up the cliff. The Boy watches closely to see what they have found. They toss things down on the ground by the cave entrance. There are berries, nuts, and white chewy roots. These will all go well with the meat. If there *is* any meat.

The sun drops low in the sky, and the Boy still waits. The shadows of the trees are crawling up to the ledge. The men should be back by now.

Yes, there they are. The Boy can hear twigs snapping in the woods. Then he sees the long spears with the stone points glinting in the sun. The men come walking out of the woods. The Boy races down to meet them.

The first two men are carrying the body of a deer. The others have nothing. It has not been a good day's hunting, but it could be worse.

Strong Arm limps over to the men with the deer. He helps them skin it and cut it up for cooking.

27

Wise Man walks over to the Boy. "Come with us," he says.

Two men have made bundles of small branches. They rub them in the fat of the dead deer. They light the torches in the fire.

Wise Man leads the way to another cave nearby. The men and the Boy go inside. One of the men with torches goes first.

They walk a long way into the cave. They have to squeeze through a narrow passage and then wade through a cold stream. The light of the torches flickers on the cave walls.

They come to a bigger part of the cave. Wise Man takes a torch and holds it close to the wall.

The Boy gasps. It's a buffalo! No, not a real buffalo. It is made of marks and colors on the wall. But it looks real!

"Buffalo tomorrow," says the Wise Man. The other men repeat the words. "Buffalo tomorrow."

The Boy is still staring at the wall. "What is it?" he asks.

"A picture. Men made it a long time ago."

"When Old Woman was young?"

"Before Old Woman was born. Before her mother was born."

The Boy feels confused. He had never thought that time could be so long. The picture was made a long time ago—but it is here now. Just marks on a wall. Yet he sees what another person drew long ago. Could *he* make marks to show what he sees? Would other people see it a long time in the future?

Wise Man puts his hand on the Boy's shoulder. "You will come with us on the hunt tomorrow," he says.

Go hunting! The Boy forgets about the picture. This is what he has been waiting for.

Go hunting at last! Now he has work to do. He is one of the men.

Point of View

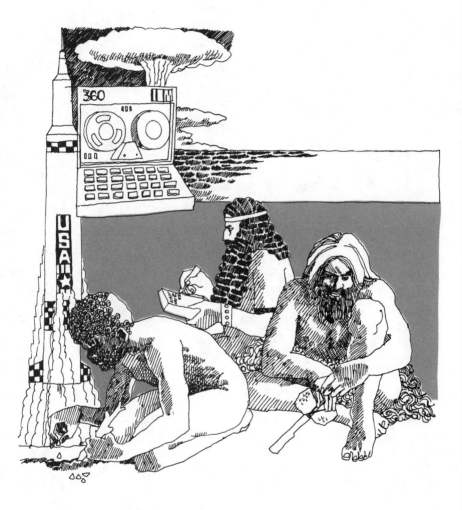

Humans have been trying to improve their lives for as long as they have been on earth. One historian wrote:

"The first hatchet, the first written message, the first seed planted in the ground were more important than such modern inventions as the atomic bomb, the computer, or the space rocket."

How do you feel about this statement? Can you think of a reason you might give for agreeing? Can you think of a reason for disagreeing? What do you think is the most important recent invention? Why?

Part 1

Mesopotamia and Egypt

Introduction: What Is Civilization?

Civilization is a difficult thing to explain. It is made up of many things we take for granted in our everyday life. Some of these things you can feel, hold, or see. Things like a road or a building.

But some things that are part of a civilization cannot be felt, held, or seen. For example, you can't touch a government, but no civilized society could last without one. You can't hold a business, a language, or family life. But civilizations would collapse without these things.

Civilization is really a way of life. In a civilized society, people do not spend most of their waking hours searching for food. Some people produce food for themselves and for other members of their community. Other people are doctors, lawyers, carpenters, storekeepers, teachers, salespeople, and so on.

Were the people we read about on pages 27-28 civilized?
They got food by hunting wild animals and by gathering

wild plants. No one knew how to farm. No one knew how to keep grazing animals.

When the wild plants were all picked and the wild animals were all killed in one area, the humans had to move to another place which had plants and animals. No one had a permanent home. Everyone moved around constantly in the search for food.

Then, about 10,000 years ago, a great turning point of history was reached. It meant that humans would be able to settle down and begin civilizations. All of human history was changed because of this discovery.

What do you think it was?

Egyptians were some of the world's earliest known farmers, as this wall painting of a harvest shows. Page 30: Sumerian statues used in religious worship.

32

Marking Time

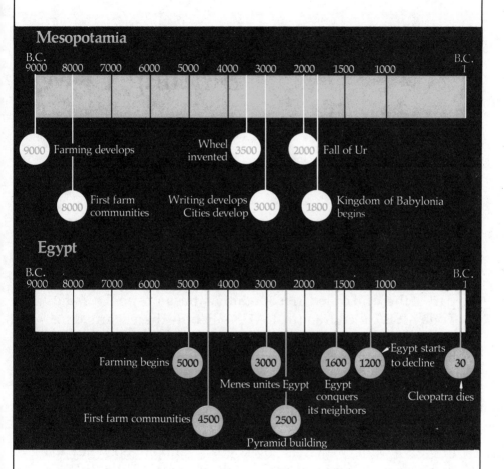

Mesopotamia

B.C. 9000 8000 7000 6000 5000 4000 3000 2000 1500 1000 — B.C. 1

- 9000 Farming develops
- 8000 First farm communities
- 3500 Wheel invented
- 3000 Writing develops / Cities develop
- 2000 Fall of Ur
- 1800 Kingdom of Babylonia begins

Egypt

B.C. 9000 8000 7000 6000 5000 4000 3000 2000 1500 1000 — B.C. 1

- 5000 Farming begins
- 4500 First farm communities
- 3000 Menes unites Egypt
- 2500 Pyramid building
- 1600 Egypt conquers its neighbors
- 1200 Egypt starts to decline
- 30 Cleopatra dies

- ■ Where did farming develop first — in Mesopotamia or in Egypt?

- ■ Which happened first: (a) the invention of the wheel in Mesopotamia, or (b) the uniting of Upper and Lower Egypt by Menes?

- ■ About what year did farming begin to develop in Mesopotamia? How many years ago was that?

- ■ How many years passed between the beginning of farming and the first Mesopotamian farm communities? Compare that with the number of years between the death of Cleopatra and today.

1

Settling Down

The experts aren't sure where it happened first. But most think that the dawn of civilization took place in the northern part of the land called Mesopotamia (mess-oh-po-TAY-me-uh). Today it is called Iraq (ih-RAHK). People there learned to grow food for themselves. They found that the seeds of wild barley and wheat grew very well when planted in the soil. All they needed was rain. And northern Mesopotamia had enough rain.

Over the years, more and more people stopped gathering wild plants. Instead they became farmers. They also learned to tame animals such as cows, goats, and sheep. They used these animals for their meat, milk, or wool. They did not have to spend the day searching for their food. They settled down in farm villages.

Times were good. The number of people in northern Mesopotamia grew. The land became crowded. Some people began to move south, to southern Mesopotamia. This area was called Sumer (SUE-mer). This land had many problems for the new settlers. The climate was very hot and dry. Without rain, nothing grew.

But two rivers ran through Sumer. They were the Tigris (TIE-gris) and the Euphrates (you-FRAY-tees) rivers. And

The Cradle of Civilization

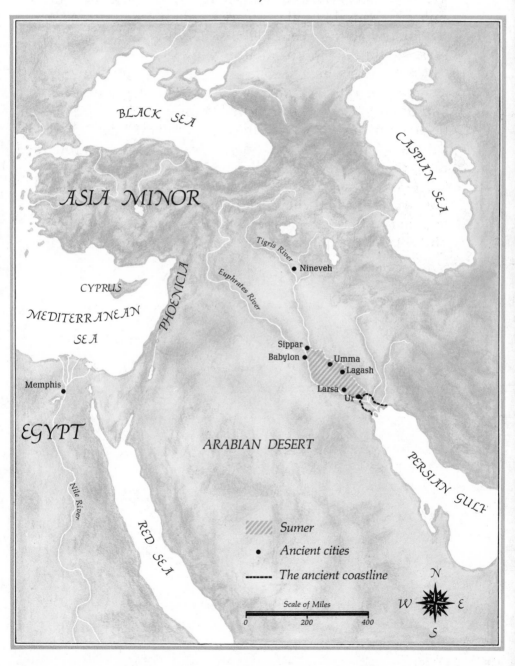

BLACK SEA

CASPIAN SEA

ASIA MINOR

Tigris River

CYPRUS

PHOENICIA

Euphrates River

• Nineveh

MEDITERRANEAN
SEA

Sippar
Babylon •   • Umma
          • Lagash
    Larsa •
        Ur •

Memphis •

EGYPT

ARABIAN DESERT

PERSIAN GULF

Nile River

RED SEA

///// Sumer

•   Ancient cities

------ The ancient coastline

Scale of Miles

0   200   400

N
W   E
S

along the rivers, there was plenty of water. Each spring these great rivers overflowed. They spilled mud on either side for miles. This muddy soil was very good for growing food. But the floods had to be controlled. Otherwise people lost their homes, and the land turned to swamps.

What did the new settlers do? They built walls along the rivers to keep them from flooding. Then they built canals and ditches across the land that connected the rivers. Water from the rivers was let into the canals and ditches. This water irrigated, or wet, the soil. Soon it was possible to grow food in all the land between the rivers.

The job of building river walls, canals, and ditches could not be done by one village alone. Several villages had to join together to build them and keep them in good condition. The villages that joined together slowly grew into large cities.

How Civilized Are You?

Imagine yourself in a spacecraft that lands on a far-off planet. You are brought before the planet's leader. He tells you that you must show you are a "civilized" person. Otherwise, you will be jailed. You begin by explaining you're from a very advanced society. After all, you've just journeyed billions of miles. Back at home, planes carry passengers at the speed of sound. Buildings rise to the heavens. Giant factories turn out thousands of goods. Giant bombs can destroy whole cities.

The leader nods his head, smiles, and then says: "These things are important. But what about the people? How do they live, and work, and spend their free time? What works of art—books, paintings, pieces of music—have your people produced? What is their attitude toward the land they live on? It is people, and their way of life, that make a society civilized."

What would you say to the planet's leader? Would you and your community pass the civilization test?

2
The Secret of the Desert

The land is a desert now. It is hot, dry, and barren. Only a few poor sheepherders live on it. Yet once this land had great cities, and the fields were green with barley and wheat. Inside the cities were the palaces of powerful kings. There were beautiful temples to honor the gods. There were schools, workshops, and homes built of bricks. There were busy, crowded marketplaces.

These were the world's first cities. They were built more than 5,000 years ago in the land of Sumer.

The people of Sumer, called Sumerians (sue-MER-ee-uns), were first with many things. They invented the wagon wheel, the plow, and the sailboat. They baked clay and mud into bricks for buildings. They melted metals such as copper and bronze, and shaped them in molds. They learned how to use numbers.

The greatest invention of the Sumerians was writing. Sumerians usually wrote on a piece of wet clay. They developed a kind of shorthand writing, called cuneiform (ku-NEE-uh-form).

Thousands of pieces of clay with cuneiform writing have been dug up from the desert. They tell us much about the life, laws, and history of Sumer. So do the ruins of Sumerian cities like Ur (er). The cities have been dug up in the last 100 years by men and women who study how people lived long ago.

The year: 1927.
The place: a desert hill in southern Iraq.

Sir Leonard Woolley and his Arab workmen dug down into the sand. Woolley believed that the great city of Ur had once stood on this spot. Its ruins were probably buried beneath the mound of sand.

Woolley guessed that he was probably digging in a burial ground of Ur. He was right. He and his men found about 2,000 graves. Nearly all were the graves of common people. The bodies were buried in the same way. Each was lying on its side, as if sleeping. Inside the coffins were beads, earrings, knives, and pins. Outside the coffins were jars of food and water, daggers, tools, mirrors, and combs. These were the things the dead would need for their trip to the next world.

Woolley also found 16 very large graves, or tombs, in which kings were buried. They were built of stone or brick, and had one or more rooms. When Woolley entered these tombs, he could hardly believe his eyes. The tombs were like underground palaces. He found not only the bones of kings, but the bones of the many people who had served them. These people had chosen to die with their kings. That's because they believed the kings were gods. The servants had entered their king's tomb alive and then swallowed a drug that made death painless. They expected that they would then be able to serve their god-kings in the next world.

One of the 16 kings' tombs was very rich. At the tomb's entrance Woolley found the bodies of six guards in two neat rows. They had copper spears and helmets. Just inside the tomb were two wagons. Each was "pulled" by three oxen. The drivers were in the wagons. The leather reins were decorated with beads of silver and rich blue stones.

The bodies of nine women were leaning against one wall of the room. They were women of the king's court. All wore head coverings of rich beads, gold leaves, and silver combs.

The king himself was buried in a smaller room with men servants. The passage leading to the door of the king's room was lined with the skeletons of soldiers. All had daggers. One had a bundle of four spears with gold heads. Two others had sets of silver spears. Robbers had broken into the king's room and stolen most of its ornaments.

The royal tombs found by Woolley in Ur were extremely old. They were built between 2700 B.C. and 2500 B.C. *What did these tombs tell Woolley about the people of Sumer at this time?*

• They were a very advanced people—skilled builders, craftsmen, and artists.

• Their kings were treated as gods and had great power and wealth.

• Their merchants traded with many lands. Sumer had no metals or stones, and very little wood. The metals, stones, and wood found in the tombs must have come from trade.

• Their soldiers had good weapons and were well trained.

• They knew how to write.

• They were ahead of all other peoples of their time.

41

Important Garbage

It is 4000 A.D., and astronauts from the planet Ur in a far-off galaxy land on the deserted planet Earth. They want to study what life must have been like 2,000 years earlier. Their history books tell them that once there was a great civilization on Earth. But in 2500 A.D. the planet became so polluted that all the humans left Earth for Ur.

The spacecraft lands in what used to be your community. Now in 4000 A.D. it is just a pile of ruined buildings and rubble. The astronauts begin digging into the rubble.

Make a list of 10 things that the astronauts would find in the rubble. Include only those things which might tell the astronauts something important about how people lived in your community in the 1970's. Explain just what each item might tell the astronaut about life in your community. For example, suppose a beer bottle or a 10-cent stamp were dug up. What would that reveal?

3

Daily Life in Sumer

By the year 3000 B.C., Sumer had about 12 great cities. They had such names as Larsa, Lagash, Umma, and Ur. The people of these cities spoke and wrote the same language, and prayed to many of the same gods. But each city ruled itself and the land around it.

The cities of Sumer were seldom at peace. They fought each other almost constantly. They fought over boundary lines, water rights, or the desire to rule the others. In times of war, a Sumerian city chose a king to lead it. When the war was over, the king was supposed to give up his power. But after a while, the kings kept their power and handed it down to their sons.

Once in a while, a great king would defeat the other cities and set up a large empire. But these empires did not last long. One or more cities would overthrow them. Then the cities would start fighting again.

The year: about 2400 B.C.

The place: the city of Lagash in Sumer.

The scene: a busy market street. Booths with all kinds of goods for sale line the mud-brick buildings. Awnings cover the booths to shade them from the hot sun.

The action: Two citizens of Lagash, Shulgi and Urgar, are walking through the market.

SHULGI: Well, Urgar, how is business? Good, I hope.

URGAR: Oh, I can't complain about business. In fact, it's better than ever. Right now I'm waiting for a shipment of cedar wood from Lebanon. Sumer can always use wood. I'll make a good profit, I'm sure.

SHULGI: Then why don't you sound happy?

URGAR: Well, Shulgi, you know how it is. You make a profit, and what happens? The king's tax collectors take it all away from you. Is there anything they don't tax today? They tax a man's cattle, the wool he cuts from his sheep, the fish in

his pond. If he can't pay, they take away his goods. In many cases, it's plain robbery. Free men must sell themselves into slavery to pay all they owe.

SHULGI: Yes, it's true. Taxes get worse every year. Why, a man even has to pay taxes when he dies. The tax collectors go to his funeral and take barley, bread, and wine from his poor widow. No wonder the king and his officials get richer while the common people get poorer You see more and more beggars in the streets every day.

URGAR: I tell you, Shulgi, it was a sad day when the kings got

45

so powerful. Once men became kings to lead us in war. When peace came, they became ordinary citizens again. But there were so many wars, the kings stayed in power. Now they hand down their power to their sons!

SHULGI: Speaking of war, Urgar, people are saying we will soon be at war again with Umma

URGAR: What is the reason this time?

SHULGI: The same old story. The king of Umma says that some of our land belongs to him. He says the people on this land should pay taxes to Umma, not to Lagash. You know what I think? I think he really wants the new canal our king built on this land, not the taxes.

URGAR: War, war, war. If it isn't war with Umma, then it's war with some other city. One year it's Larsa, then it's Ur, then it's Umma all over again. Do you know what I think, Shulgi? If the cities of Sumer do not unite, they will die. All around us are barbarians [bar-BEAR-ee-uhnz; people believed to be uncivilized]. They would like nothing better than to take over our rich fields and cities. If we keep fighting each other, the barbarians will destroy us some day.

SHULGI: Nonsense, Urgar. You worry too much. I'm a writer. I have gone to school. I know more about such things than you. How can such poor, ignorant people ever defeat us?

URGAR: I hope you are right, Shulgi. I'll tell you this: My shipment of wood had better arrive soon. If war with Umma breaks out, I'll never get the shipment. I'll be ruined.

SHULGI: Urgar, you need to have some fun and relax. How about watching the wrestling matches over in the square? There's going to be a big crowd today, so let's hurry and get good seats.

URGAR: A good idea, Shulgi.

Who Is Right?

Shulgi and Urgar are writing to friends who live in neighboring towns. Examine their letters and decide (a) which was written by Shulgi, which by Urgar, and (b) which letter better describes the future of Lagash and other Sumerian cities.

Dear friend,
   Don't be alarmed by rumors that the end is near for Sumer. Why, our armies are the best in the world. Those poor, ignorant hill tribes will never defeat us. Besides, it's not good to worry so much. My advice is — relax and enjoy yourself.

Dear friend,
   Sumer is doomed. The kings are too powerful. The taxes are too high. The cities fight each other for no reason. If things continue this way, the desert and hill people will soon be able to destroy us completely.

4

The Fall of the Kingdom

What finally happened to the great cities of Sumer? Sumer was a flat land, open to attack from almost every side. All around it were rough tribesmen, mainly poor sheepherders. These outsiders were jealous of the rich cities and fields of the Sumerians. They often attacked the Sumerian cities. Usually the Sumerians were able to defeat them. But by about 2200 B.C., the Sumerian cities had become weak from constant fighting. Their enemies had become stronger. Soon the enemies began to take over the cities of Sumer. The last great city, Ur, was taken about 2000 B.C.

King Ibbi-Sin of Ur was in great trouble. Desert tribesmen were outside the walls of his city. They were getting ready to attack it. The brick wall around Ur was thick and strong. But the supply of food in the city was getting low. Food prices had gone way up. Fish and barley were selling at 50 times the usual price. Many people were starving. How long could the city hold out?

King Ibbi-Sin had written to his governors and begged for help. He needed both food and soldiers. But the governors took advantage of his weakness. Many refused to obey him any longer. One governor made a deal with Ibbi-Sin. He would send help if Ibbi-Sin would make him king of two

cities. Ibbi-Sin agreed and made him king. But no help came. Instead, the new king began to take over other cities.

At last the tribesmen broke into Ur and took Ibbi-Sin away as a prisoner. Then they destroyed the great city and its temple. A poet of Sumer wrote a *lament* (a sad poem) about the fall of Ur. This is part of it:

The walls of Ur were broken: The people mourn . . .
At the tall gates, where people liked to walk, dead bodies lay about.
In its wide streets, where feasts were held, scattered they lay. . . .
Corpses, like fat placed in the sun, melted away. . . .
The old men and women who could not leave their houses were
   overcome by fire.
The babies lying in their mothers' laps were carried off. . . .
Our way of life perished. The people mourn.

Why Did It Happen?

Three Sumerian soldiers who had been taken prisoner were discussing the reasons for the defeat of their city. One soldier said, "Ur fell because our king was too weak." Another said, "Ur fell because the noblemen were only interested in gaining more power for themselves." The third said, "You're both wrong; Ur fell because the enemy invaders were just stronger than the Sumerians." If you had been part of that discussion, whose opinion would you have supported? Or do you think each man was right in his own way? Do you think there was any way that Ur could have been saved?

5

Hammurabi's Code

The fall of Ur marked the end of the Sumerians as a people. The cities of Sumer were taken over by the neighboring tribes. These invaders, who were desert herders, soon became city people themselves. They copied the ways of the Sumerians, especially their religion, law, and arts. They made the city of Babylon (BAB-uh-lun) their capital. They built a new and united empire called Babylonia (bab-uh-LO-nee-uh). One of the greatest of the kings of Babylon was Hammurabi (HAM-uh-RAHB-ee). His famous Code of Laws was one of the first sets of laws used to rule a kingdom.

The place: the city of Sippar (sip-AR) on the Euphrates River.

The time: about 1700 B.C.

The scene: the city courthouse. Three judges are sitting at one end of the courtroom. Near them is the clerk of the court. He writes on slabs of wet clay. He makes marks in them with a thin knife.

CHIEF JUDGE: What's the first case?

CLERK: The merchant Dagan, my lord.

(A man steps forward from the other end of the room.)

CHIEF JUDGE: What's your complaint?

DAGAN: My lord, I carry goods up and down the river on boats. My dock is close to the temple. Ten days ago, one of my boats arrived at the dock. It had a load of timber from Tultul (tool-tool). It was—

JUDGE UBAR *(holding a hand to his ear)*: A load of what from where?

DAGAN: Timber, my lord. For building. And it was from Tultul, up the river.

CHIEF JUDGE: Go on.

DAGAN: Well, my slaves started unloading the boat. Just then I saw another boat coming down the river. It was out of control. It crashed into my boat. And my boat tipped over. The timber floated away. I lost it all.

CHIEF JUDGE: And you blame the owner of the other boat?

DAGAN: Yes, I do. I have read the Code of Hammurabi. There is a law about a case like this. It says the owner of the other boat must pay for the loss.

CHIEF JUDGE: True. But the Code is meant to guide us. We must not follow it blindly. Is the owner of the other boat here?

(A man steps forward.)

NABSA: Y-yes, my lord. I am Nabsa. But it wasn't my fault. I—

CHIEF JUDGE: Calm down, man. Now tell your story.

NABSA: My lord, I was taking *bally* to *Barbylon*.

JUDGE UBAR: You were taking what to where?

NABSA *(nervously)*: I mean, barley to Babylon. The boat had just started when I saw water coming in. There was a leak in the boat. I called to the boatmen to plug it. And that's when we ran into the other boat.

CHIEF JUDGE: You were unlucky. But it was still your fault. You didn't look where you were going.

NABSA: Excuse me, my lord. The boat was not well built. I too have read the Code of Hammurabi. It says the builder of a boat must guarantee it for one year. If it breaks down, he must pay for the loss.

CHIEF JUDGE: So the leak was the boat builder's fault?

NABSA: Yes, my lord. And I bought it only two moons ago.

CHIEF JUDGE: Is the boat builder here?

(Another man steps forward.)

LUSHU: My name is Lushu, my lord. I built the boat for the merchant Nabsa. But I built it well. If there was a leak, it was his fault. He must have run it on rocks.

CHIEF JUDGE: First of all, one thing is clear. The merchant Dagan will get damages. He will be paid for his timber. The question is, who is to pay? Nabsa or Lushu?

LUSHU: My lord, is this right? There is nothing in the Code about a boat builder paying someone who didn't buy his boat.

CHIEF JUDGE: No. But the idea behind the laws is quite clear. If the leak was your fault, you will have to pay.

LUSHU: It was not *my* fault.

NABSA: It was not *my* fault.

CHIEF JUDGE: Then you both must take an oath in the temple. Will you swear by the gods that you are innocent? Lushu, what about you?

LUSHU: Yes, my lord. I am willing to take the oath.

CHIEF JUDGE: And you, Nabsa?

NABSA *(clearing his throat):* Well, my lord, I . . . er . . . I mean, I did run the boat on some rocks once. I don't think it made the leak. But I can't take an oath on it.

(The Chief Judge looks at the other judges. They nod.)

CHIEF JUDGE: Very well. Nabsa, you will pay damages to Dagan.

(Nabsa, Dagan, and Lushu bow to the judges and walk out.)

JUDGE UBAR *(shaking his head):* All these merchants rushing around in boats. No wonder there are so many accidents.

Front Page

The five headlines below could have appeared in the newspapers of Mesopotamia—if Mesopotamia had ever had newspapers. Your job is to arrange the headlines in their proper order on another sheet. Put the event that happened first at the top, and so on. Then, for each headline, write a one-paragraph "news story." The story should tell what happened and why the event was important.

BARBARIAN TRIBES OVERRUN SUMER; UR REPORTED CAPTURED

Hammurabi Issues Code of Justice; Says Law Is Now "Eye for Eye"

Lagash and Ur at War Again; King Says War Necessary "To Preserve Way of Life"

ENGLISH EXPERT DIGS IN DESERT FOR RUINS OF UR; SOME SAY HE'S HAD TOO MUCH SUN

Woman Puts Seed in Ground; Six Months Afterwards: A New Plant Discovered; Experts Are Amazed

6
Gift of the Nile

"It has wonders more than any other land. It has works so great that they cannot be described."

A Greek writer of history, named Herodotus, said this about Egypt in the fifth century B.C. He had seen many great wonders in his time. But nothing he saw compared with Egypt's great pyramids. The pyramids were already 2,000 years old when Herodotus saw them. They are still standing today, 2,500 years later. They may last forever.

Why was Egypt able to make such great buildings so long ago? Egypt was a very fortunate land. It had the Nile River. This river starts in central Africa and flows 4,000 miles north to the Mediterranean Sea. Most of Egypt was, and still is, a hot, dry, barren desert. But late every summer the Nile overflowed in Egypt and flooded the land. It left a layer of rich mud that was good for growing food. That was the "gift of the Nile."

During the growing season, the sides of the Nile are green with wheat and barley. This strip of green land is usually from eight to 13 miles wide. From the air, the Nile looks like a narrow ribbon of green winding through the pink desert. Almost all Egyptians live on this narrow strip of land.

Farming along the Nile was risky, just as it was along the Tigris and Euphrates. If the Nile overflowed too much, villages

Along the Nile River, families often worked together as a team. This tomb painting shows Egyptian families hunting geese with sticks.

were covered by water. If it overflowed too little, not much land could be planted. Then people went hungry.

The Egyptians began to build dikes (walls) to control the Nile. They dug large holes that filled with water when the river overflowed. Then they built canals and ditches to carry this water into the fields. They also drained swamps.

As in Sumer, villages had to join together to do this work. Gradually cities began to form with governments to rule them. In Sumer the cities fought against each other constantly. But Egypt became a united nation, the first in history. About 3100 B.C., a king from south Egypt defeated the north and joined the two lands into one. This king, Menes (MEE-nees), was the first of Egypt's many pharaohs (FAIR-ohs), rulers who were believed to be gods. Under the rule of the pharaohs, Egypt became a great nation that lasted 3,000 years.

Ancient Egypt

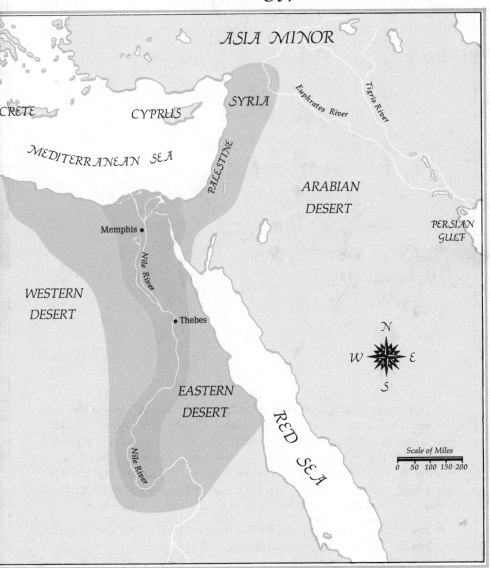

ASIA MINOR

CRETE

CYPRUS

SYRIA

Euphrates River

Tigris River

MEDITERRANEAN SEA

PALESTINE

ARABIAN
DESERT

PERSIAN
GULF

Memphis

WESTERN
DESERT

Nile River

Thebes

N
W   E
S

EASTERN
DESERT

RED SEA

Nile River

Scale of Miles
0   50 100 150 200

Under Egypt's direct control, 1450 B.C.   Egyptian influence, 1450 B.C.

Village Planning

The drawing above shows an ancient Egyptian village on the Nile River. The squares are the homes of the villagers. The triangles are the hills lying to the south of the town. The arrows show the direction in which the Nile flows. The dots show areas that will flood in the rainy season. You are an Egyptian villager. You know that the Nile is going to flood its banks within the next two weeks. In this period you must build a dike, an irrigation canal, and a village well.

■ Your village has time to build only one dike before the flooding begins. Where will you put it?

■ You have time to build only one well for all the villagers to use. Where will you locate it?

■ Where will you dig the irrigation canals? Be prepared to defend your answers in class.

7

The Gods of Egypt

The people of Egypt had many gods who, they believed, ruled their lives. These gods often took strange forms. One god, Bes (behs), had the body of a dwarf and the head of a lion. He was supposed to scare off evil spirits.

The most popular Egyptian god was Osiris (oh-SEAR-is), the god of the dead. Wealthy Egyptians spent much time and money preparing for death. Yet the Egyptians were not a gloomy people. They believed strongly in life after death. This afterlife would be a happy one, just as life on earth was. And, according to the Egyptians, Osiris was the god who had made life after death possible.

The Egyptians believed that Osiris had once ruled Egypt as a king in human form. Osiris had taught them to plant food and made them civilized. But Osiris had a brother, Seth, who was jealous of him. Seth locked Osiris in a box and threw it into the Nile. Later he cut the body of Osiris into 14 pieces and scattered them.

Osiris had a sister, Isis (EYE-sis), who loved him. She searched the swamps of the Nile for the pieces of his body. She found them all, and then wept for her young brother. According to the legend, the sun god, Re (ray), heard her crying. He pitied

61

For Egyptians, the god Osiris (left) was a symbol
of life after death. Behind him in this tomb
painting stands the jackal-headed god who put
Osiris back together. The third figure is Osiris' son.

Isis, and sent down a god from heaven to help her. This god, who had the head of a jackal, fitted the pieces of Osiris together. Then he and Isis wrapped the body in linen bandages and prayed for it. Osiris rose from the dead and became king in the next world.

The Egyptians saw in the story of Osiris the promise of life after death. They believed that they too could rise from the dead if their bodies were treated in the same way. This meant making *mummies* of their bodies. How was an Egyptian mummy made? First the dead body was treated with salts, spices, and resins to dry and shrink it. Then it was completely wrapped with layers of linen bandages to preserve it. The family of the dead person wept, and priests said prayers. Finally, the mummy was put inside a stone tomb. Food, clothes, and furniture were also put inside the tomb. It was thought that the dead person would need these in the afterlife.

Only wealthy Egyptians could afford to be buried in this way. But even poor Egyptians prepared themselves for life after death. They were usually buried in sand graves with scraps of food and tools.

Osiris was thought to be the god who brought the dead back to life. The Egyptians believed that he gave new life not only to people, but to the land as well. How did Osiris make the land come alive? During the summer, Egypt was so dry that nothing could grow in the soil. Even the sides of the Nile were bare. The land was dead. But late in the summer the Nile began to rise and finally to overflow. The Egyptians believed that the tears of Isis, crying for Osiris, made the river flood. By November the flood waters went back to the Nile. But now the sides of the river were wet with mud again. This was the time to plant food.

The story of Osiris gave the Egyptians hope. It gave them hope that each year food would grow again along the Nile. And it gave them hope of everlasting life after death.

Egypt's Gods

In the chart below, the left-hand column contains statements about the Egyptian god Osiris. The center column asks questions relating to the statement. The right-hand column asks for your interpretation. What do you think are the answers to these questions?

The Statement	The Question	The Interpretation
According to legend, Osiris was an Egyptian king. His people loved him.	Why?	?
His brother, Seth, killed Osiris, cut up his body, and threw the pieces into the Nile.	Why did Seth do that?	?
His sister, Isis, searched and found the pieces of the body. She sat at the river and cried for her dead brother.	What did the Egyptians believe the tears of Isis did to the Nile River?	?
Osiris rose from the dead.	According to the legend, how did that happen?	?
The legend of Osiris made death seem less frightening to the Egyptians.	What could Egyptians now hope for when they died?	?

8

Building the Pyramids

The pyramids of Egypt are one of the great wonders of the world. Most of the buildings of the ancient world have crumbled, but some of the mighty pyramids still stand. They line the western side of the Nile River in northern Egypt. The pyramids are solid stone buildings. They have a square base and sides shaped like triangles that meet in a point at the top.

How were these enormous buildings built? Why were they built? For thousands of years after the fall of Egypt, people were not really sure. Now we know enough about the ancient Egyptians to answer these questions.

The year: about 2600 B.C:
The place: the west side of the Nile at Gîza (GHEE-zuh).

The great blocks of stone weighed more than two tons each. Gangs of men strained to pull them up the high ramp. Egypt did not have horses or wheels yet. The stones were tied on flat wooden sleds and pulled with ropes. The stones moved by inches. The sun was burning hot, but the men could not stop to rest. They were whipped if they did. Finally the heavy stones had to be lifted up and set into place. The work could break a man's back.

These men were working on the Great Pyramid at Gîza. It was, and still is, the largest stone building in the world.

It is made up of more than two million stones. It is as tall as a 45-story building of today.

Like other pyramids, it was built as a tomb for the pharaoh. The pharaoh of Egypt was considered to be a god who owned the nation and everything in it. Everyone in Egypt had to serve the god-king. The pharaoh Cheops (KEE-ops) drafted 100,000 men a year to build the Great Pyramid. It took 20 years to finish.

How was the Great Pyramid built? First a perfect square was measured in the desert. Then the sand was cleared from this square. Below the sand was solid rock that had to be leveled. The pyramid would be built on this rock.

Meanwhile, other workers were cutting some blocks from rocky desert cliffs. Sometimes they were a long way from Gîza. Then the stones would be put on logs and rolled to the edge of the Nile. There they were loaded onto barges and rowed down the river. At Gîza, they were mounted on sleds and pulled up ramps on each side of the pyramid. When put in place, each stone fit exactly on top of the stone below.

The pyramid was solid stone except for the king's room and the low, narrow tunnels leading to it. The tunnels were blocked with large stones so the pharaoh's mummy would be safe. But tomb robbers were able to break in. They stole the mummy to get its jewels.

Why did Cheops and other pharaohs build their tombs in the shape of pyramids? A sentence written in one of these tombs gives a clue. It says, "A staircase to heaven is laid for the pharaoh so that he may mount up to heaven on it." The pyramids, sloping high up to the sky, were "staircases to heaven." From them, Egyptians believed, the pharaohs could join the sun god, Re, and travel with him across the sky. Any time they wished, they could go back to their tombs. There, it was thought, they would enjoy the food and drink which had been put out for them by the priests. Egypt's god-kings built the pyramids to use in their everlasting life after death.

What's Wrong Here?

The picture below shows workers in old Egypt building the pyramids. If you examine the picture carefully, you'll find that some items just don't belong. For example, metal cranes were not known during the ancient Egyptian period. On a sheet of paper, number from one to ten. List all the things you see wrong with the picture.

9

The Queen Who Tried To Save Egypt

For more than a thousand years, Egypt was a proud and powerful nation. The people thought that their country would remain powerful forever. But it didn't.

Around 1200 B.C. hard times came to Egypt. Law, order, and justice left the land. Bandits robbed peaceful workers almost every day. High prices brought misery to the peasants. Many Egyptians began robbing the sacred tombs of the pharaohs.

The leaders of Egypt did little to help. They were too busy stuffing their own pockets with gold. Before long, the land of Egypt became divided and weak. It was easily defeated by the armies of other nations. The once-proud empire of Egypt fell. It became a part of other, greater empires. Finally, in 332 B.C., it was swallowed up by Greece.

A 17-year-old Greek girl became queen of Egypt in 51 B.C. Her name was Cleopatra (klee-uh-PA-truh). Cleopatra wanted to make Egypt strong again. The big problem was Rome. The Romans had built a powerful empire. Now they had their eyes on Egypt.

Cleopatra spent her life struggling for her country. In the end, she lost — and killed herself. But her struggle made her one of the most famous women in history. She is the heroine of many books, plays, and movies. Here is her story.

Cleopatra is sitting in the royal bedroom. A maid combs her hair. Another maid smooths out her royal dress.

The summer sun burns down on the palace in Alexandria (al-ig-ZAN-dree-uh), Egypt's capital city. There is a breeze in the palace gardens. But Cleopatra cannot go outside. A guard stands at the door. Her enemy, the Roman leader Octavian (ock-TAY-vee-un), has captured Egypt.

Cleopatra is thinking of two other Roman leaders. First there was Julius Caesar (SEE-zer), the Roman ruler. She had met him 18 years ago. . . .

She liked Julius Caesar from the start. And he liked Cleopatra. She was 21 and beautiful. He also saw that she was strong and smart. He thought she was a good queen.

Caesar took Cleopatra to Rome. She stayed there for more than a year. Some Romans didn't like her "foreign ways." They were afraid she had too much influence on Caesar.

There were also some Romans who did not like Caesar. They thought he was becoming too powerful. In 44 B.C., they stabbed him to death (see page 166).

Cleopatra went back to Egypt. Rome was torn by civil war. Two men who had been friends of Caesar became its leaders. Octavian ruled the western half of the empire. The eastern half went to Marc Antony. . . .

Cleopatra opens a small box and takes out a silver coin. Her own face is on one side. Antony's is on the other.

Together, they might have ruled the Western world. Everything had seemed possible when they first met at Antony's headquarters. . . .

Antony set up his headquarters not far from Egypt. He asked Cleopatra to visit him. He hoped to get some of Egypt's wealth to supply his army. She hoped to get his support. They both got more than they hoped for. They became partners and lovers.

Cleopatra found that Antony was a strong and honest man.
Unlike most Romans, he enjoyed a good laugh—even against
himself. One day he wanted to show Cleopatra he was an expert
fisherman. He took some fish that had already been caught. Then
he got a servant to swim underwater and put them on his hook.
Cleopatra saw through the trick. So she got one of her servants
to swim there first—with a salted fish from the kitchen.

But life wasn't all play. Antony had to protect his part of the
empire against invaders. He had to settle quarrels between local
kings. Then he and Cleopatra had to face the biggest threat of all.

Octavian wanted to rule all of Rome's empire by himself.
He did all he could to turn the Romans against Antony. He built
up a powerful army. In 32 B.C. he declared war on Cleopatra.

Antony and Cleopatra didn't have a big enough army. They
lost a sea battle. Then Octavian invaded Egypt. His army reached
the suburbs of Alexandria. Antony fought fiercely and held the
invaders back.

But he knew he had lost the war. Someone told him Cleopatra
had killed herself. He thrust his sword into his chest. But Cleopatra
was still alive. Antony was carried to her and died in her arms.

Octavian marched into the city. . . .

Cleopatra raises her head. She hears a man talking to the
guard at the door.

"It's just a basket of figs for her majesty. Here, take one."
The guard lets the man in.

Cleopatra goes to sit on her golden bed. The basket is brought
to her. She knows there is something else in the basket
besides figs. She pushes her arm down among the figs.

There is a brief stabbing pain. Cleopatra has asked her
servants to hide a poisonous snake under the fruit. The snake
has done its job.

Cleopatra lies down on her bed and waits for the end. It
is not just the end of her life. It is also the end of a kingdom.

Egypt now belongs to Rome.

Front Page

The four headlines below could have appeared in an Egyptian newspaper—if ancient Egypt had ever had newspapers. Your job is to arrange the headlines in proper order on another sheet. Put the event that happened first at the top, and so on. Then for each headline, write a one-paragraph "news story." The story should tell what happened and why the event was important.

CLEOPATRA DEAD; EGYPTIAN QUEEN TAKES OWN LIFE

Egyptian Nomads Settle on Banks of Nile River, Say: "No More Wandering for Us"

UPPER AND LOWER EGYPT UNITED UNDER MENES; TWO REGIONS TO HAVE JUST ONE PHARAOH

Pharaoh Cheops To Begin Building of Great Pyramid; Some Egyptians Wondering: "Will the Desert Be Ruined?"

Part 2

The Hebrews and Phoenicians

Introduction: The Spread of Civilization

Most experts now believe that civilization began in the ancient Middle East. In Mesopotamia and Egypt, people first settled down in farming communities. They learned to irrigate land, formed governments, and developed writing.

As the years passed, these ideas spread to peoples who lived near Mesopotamia and Egypt. These peoples also formed societies, built large cities, developed art, and carried on trade.

Two of these peoples are especially important to us. The Phoenicians (fi-NISH-ens) were one. The others were the Hebrews. Both of these peoples lived about midway between Mesopotamia and Egypt (see map, page 76).

The Phoenicians were important because they were great traders and sailors. They carried goods and ideas far and wide. They visited all the lands around the Mediterranean Sea. They even sailed as far as Britain. The Phoenicians are also important because they helped in the growth of our written language. The Phoenicians developed an alphabet which is like the alphabet we use today.

Ancient Phoenicia and Palestine

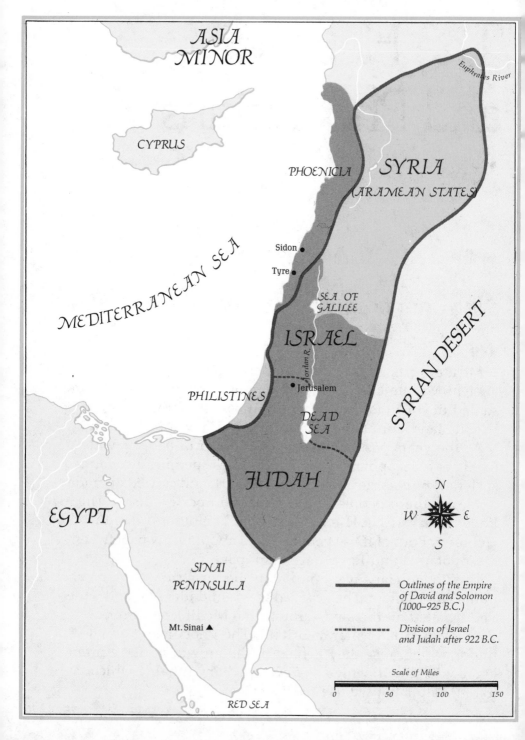

ASIA MINOR

CYPRUS

PHOENICIA

SYRIA
(ARAMEAN STATES)

Euphrates River

Sidon

Tyre

MEDITERRANEAN SEA

SEA OF GALILEE

ISRAEL

Jordan R.

PHILISTINES

Jerusalem

DEAD SEA

SYRIAN DESERT

JUDAH

EGYPT

SINAI PENINSULA

Mt. Sinai ▲

RED SEA

N
W   E
S

Outlines of the Empire
of David and Solomon
(1000–925 B.C.)

Division of Israel
and Judah after 922 B.C.

Scale of Miles

0   50   100   150

The Hebrews were small in numbers. But they were large in importance. The religion of Judaism (JOO-dah-is-um) was started by the ancient Hebrews. That religion lives on today in Israel, in the United States, and in many other countries of the West and the Middle East.

Before the Hebrews, most people practiced religions that would seem strange to us today. Most ancient peoples did not believe in One God. They had many gods. They might have a god of the sea, a god of wisdom, a god of wind, a god of love, a god of war, and so on.

The Hebrews had just One God. At first they believed that they alone lived under God's protection as His chosen people But as time went on, this idea broadened. The Hebrews came to believe that their God was the God of all people and all nations. He was the God of the whole universe.

Today, the belief in One God is held by Jews, by Christians, and by Moslems. The ancient Hebrews had other beliefs which are held by many people today. Among these beliefs:

• *God has set down laws for people to obey. These laws are called the Ten Commandments. They were given by God to the Hebrew leader, Moses.*

• *God is merciful. If a person asks God to forgive, and if that person then lives an honorable life, God will show mercy.*

• *The brotherhood of all people. Be fair to others, for all people are brothers and sisters on this earth.*

These are some of the most important values and beliefs in Western civilization today. Unfortunately, they are not always followed.

Map at left shows ancient Phoenicia and Palestine. Which of the three was largest in area—Israel, Judah, or Phoenicia? Which had the most access to the Mediterranean Sea? Page 74: One of the key figures in all of history was the Hebrew leader Moses. In this wall sculpture he is shown receiving the Ten Commandments from the hand of God.

Marking Time

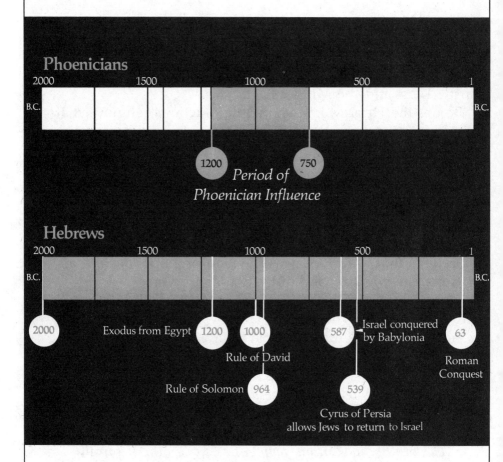

Phoenicians

2000   1500   1000   500   1

B.C.   B.C.

1200   750

*Period of
Phoenician Influence*

Hebrews

2000   1500   1000   500   1

B.C.   B.C.

2000   Exodus from Egypt   1200   1000   587   Israel conquered by Babylonia   63

Rule of David

Rule of Solomon   964   539   Roman Conquest

Cyrus of Persia
allows Jews to return to Israel

- According to the timeline, for about how many years were the Phoenicians important traders in the Mediterranean area?

- At about the same time that the Phoenicians started to develop their influence, what important event was taking place among the Hebrews?

- Which Hebrew king ruled closest to the present, David or Solomon?

- Cyrus freed the Hebrews from Babylonian rule in 539 B.C. How many years ago was that from our own time?

1

The Phoenicians

The Phoenicians were the greatest sailors, adventurers, and traders of their time. For 300 years, their ships carried much of the trade in the Mediterranean Sea. They brought the fine goods of the Middle East and Egypt to the peoples of Europe. They brought to Europe something even more valuable. This was the alphabet, which they probably adapted from earlier Middle Eastern languages.

The Phoenicians lived on a narrow strip of land on the east coast of the Mediterranean. Their homeland was part of what is now Lebanon and Syria. In front of them was the sea. Behind them were tall mountains. There was little land for farming. So the Phoenicians turned to the Mediterranean as a way of making a living.

At first they sailed their small ships close to shore, and only by day. At night they put their ships on beaches. But later they built larger ships, and learned to sail at night by the stars.

By 1100 B.C. they were masters of the sea. They began sailing boldly to strange lands. They sailed to Greece, Italy, North Africa, Spain, Britain, and the west coast of Africa. They started colonies or trading posts in all of these different places.

The Phoenicians were not looking for glory. They were looking for trade. Often they did not understand the language of the people they met. But that did not stop the Phoenicians from making deals. An ancient writer tells how the Phoenicians traded in West Africa:

"When they arrive, they unload their goods on the beach. Then they go back to their ship and send up a smoke signal. The natives see the smoke and come down to the shore. They then put down as much gold as they think the goods are worth. The Phoenicians come ashore and look at the gold. If they think the gold is enough, they take it and go their way. But if it does not seem enough, they go back to their ship again and wait. Then the natives approach and add to the gold until the Phoenicians are content. Both sides are fair. The Phoenicians never touch the gold until it matches the worth of their goods. And the natives never carry off the goods until the gold is taken away."

The Phoenicians were good businessmen and kept careful records of their deals. But to do this, they had to have a good system of writing. Both the Egyptian and Sumerian systems were hard to learn and use. So the Phoenicians adapted another system, which contained an alphabet. Their letters, much changed in form, make up most of the alphabet that we use today. The Phoenicians taught this alphabet to the Greeks, who added the vowel letters to it. This simple alphabet spread the art of writing in the Western world.

Handwriting on the Wall

Drawing by Ed Fisher; © 1963
The New Yorker Magazine, Inc.

"It doesn't mean a thing, but boy, will it drive them crazy a thousand years from now!"

- What is the point of this cartoon?
- Why did the Phoenicians need a system of writing?
- How did the Phoenicians pass their writing on to other parts of the world?

2

The Great Escape

It is the greatest escape story of all time. It is the story of the Hebrews' escape from slavery in Egypt. The story is told in the Bible's Old Testament, which is a history of the early Hebrews. It is not written the way history is written today. The Hebrews saw their escape from Egypt as an act of God, and they gave all credit to His miraculous powers. Their story is written in the language of faith, rather than history. It is often a poetic story. Yet the events it tells about—the slavery of the Hebrews in Egypt and their escape—are true. This is the story:

The Hebrews came from an area near Ur. They first settled in the land of Canaan (KAY-nun), or Palestine, along the east coast of the Mediterranean Sea. A long period without rain brought hunger and suffering to many of the Hebrews. The tribe of Jacob, a grandson of Abraham, left Palestine and went to Egypt. In Egypt, the Nile overflowed every year, and there was enough water for their sheep and cattle.

*In Egypt, Hebrew slaves were forced to do field work
and to labor "in mortar and brick" for pharaohs
such as Ramses the Second (shown in statue at right).*

The members of this group were known as Israelites. When
they went to Egypt, that country was ruled by foreigners.
These foreigners were friendly with the Israelites. But the
Egyptians, led by their own pharaoh, drove out the foreigners.
Then the Egyptians wanted revenge against the Israelites too.

Most of the Hebrews became slaves. They had to do hard
work, building cities for the pharaohs. This is what the Old
Testament says about their slavery:

"The Egyptians feared the people of Israel. They made
their lives bitter with hard work, in mortar and brick, and
in all kinds of work in the fields."

84

The Hebrews were slaves in Egypt for about 300 years. Finally, a Hebrew leader named Moses began to plead with the pharaoh for their freedom. Who was Moses?

The Old Testament says that the daughter of a pharaoh found Moses when he was a baby. She took pity on the Hebrew child and raised him herself. After Moses had grown up, he saw an Egyptian beating two Hebrew slaves. He killed the Egyptian and then ran away from the pharaoh's court.

The Old Testament says that God told Moses to go to the pharaoh and say, "Let my people go." When the pharaoh refused, God punished Egypt in awful ways. Egypt was overrun by frogs, flies, and locusts; many Egyptians died. Finally, the pharaoh agreed to let the Hebrews go.

We know for sure that Moses *did* lead the Hebrews out of Egypt. The shortest way was the road along the Mediterranean coast. This led directly to the "promised land" of Palestine. But there were many Egyptian soldiers along this road and it was unsafe for the Hebrews. Instead, Moses may have led them across some shallow swamps and into the Sinai (SIGH-nigh) desert. The Hebrews called these swamps the "Sea of Reeds" because of the tall grass that grew in them. It may be that the Sea of Reeds was later called the Red Sea by mistake.

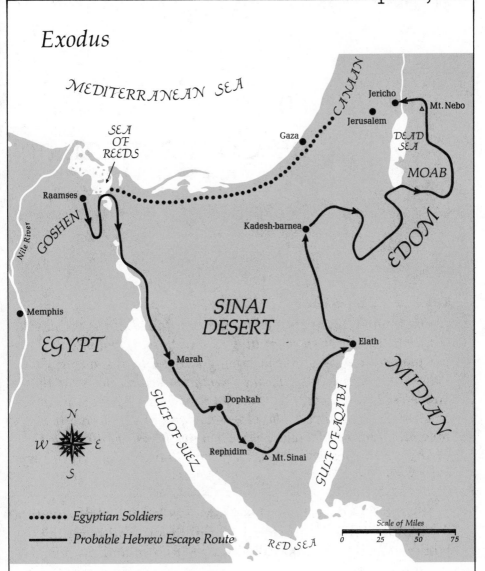

Exodus

- In what direction is Canaan from Egypt?

- As the Hebrews journeyed back to Canaan, what kind of land were they crossing?

- The Hebrews could have taken a shorter route back to Canaan. Why did they decide not to use that route? Use a piece of string and the scale of miles to measure about how many miles the Hebrews would have traveled along the exodus route shown on the map.

3

The Commandments

The Hebrews who escaped from Egypt found life in the desert very hard. They often went hungry and thirsty, and many complained to Moses. But according to the Old Testament, God heard their complaints and once again worked miracles for the Hebrews. Before long, they had both food and water. Still, their troubles were not over. The desert was full of wandering tribes who attacked the Hebrews. The Hebrews fought battles against their enemies and won. They were sure that God had given them their victories.

Now, the Old Testament says, Moses led the Hebrews to a rocky hill in the desert called Mount Sinai. And here, the Hebrews believed, God called Moses to him and proposed a solemn agreement.

God reminded Moses that He, the Lord, had saved the Hebrews from the Egyptians. Now they had a duty to obey Him. If they did, they would be His special, or chosen, people. They would lead other peoples of the world to believe in the One True God.

Moses and the Hebrews accepted this agreement with the Lord. It became the foundation of their faith. Then the Lord gave Moses His laws, which the Hebrews had to obey. These laws are called the Ten Commandments. This is what they say:

1. You shall have no other gods before me.
2. You shall not make any pictures, statues, or images for purposes of worship.
3. You shall not take the name of the Lord your God in vain.
4. Remember the Sabbath day to keep it holy.
5. Honor your father and your mother.
6. You shall not commit murder.
7. You shall not commit adultery.
8. You shall not steal.
9. You shall not bear false witness against your neighbor.
10. You shall not desire what belongs to your neighbor.

The faith of the Hebrews was unlike any other of their time. The Hebrews believed there were no gods—only God. He was not just the God of the Hebrews. He was the God of every people and all nations, the Creator of the universe. The Hebrews saw God behind all events in history; God *made* history. And finally, they saw themselves as a special people chosen to bring the Word of God to others.

Carving of a Menorah, a candle holder used in Jewish religious services.

Justice in the Desert

Imagine you are an ancient Hebrew in the Sinai desert. Your people live by the Ten Commandments. However, a number of people are accused of violating the Commandments. Do you think they did so?

- Aaron is a farmer. He prays to the Hebrew God every day. But it hasn't rained in months, and his neighbors caught him doing a rain dance to an Egyptian god.

- Benjamin and Eric are neighbors. Benjamin's tent is bigger and more luxurious than Eric's. Eric's wife, Sharon, keeps complaining that she wants a tent like Benjamin's.

- Ezra is a baker. He says he can't attend prayer sessions on the Sabbath because he has to do his baking. After all, nobody wants to buy stale cakes.

- Seth is 12 years old. He has been lame in one leg since birth. He refuses to help his mother bring water from the oasis. He refuses to help his father tend the sheep. He often stays out late even though his father has warned him to be home before dark.

4
David's City

The Hebrews' homeland was rough country. They lived in the rocky hills of Palestine. Many kept sheep for a living. They moved about, looking for fresh grass for their animals.

The Hebrews were divided into 12 tribes. Each of the tribes went its own way. But they had one thing in common: belief in their God.

Other peoples lived in Palestine, mostly in the valleys. Often there was war between these peoples and the Hebrews. They fought for living space. The Hebrews realized that they could fight better if all their tribes joined together. To do that, they needed a leader. At first they united under a king known as Saul. Then, when Saul was killed in battle, they had to find another man whom all would respect.

There was a man named David. He had once kept sheep. He liked to play music and sing songs. He was a tough soldier. People admired him. And just about 3,000 years ago, David became king of the Hebrews.

David believed his people should have a capital city. But he did not want to pick a place belonging to one of the 12 tribes. That would be like playing favorites. Instead, he chose a foreign city in the middle of the Hebrews' land. It was called Jerusalem.

First he had to get hold of the city. It stood on top of a hill and was guarded by thick stone walls. The people in the city laughed at David. No one had ever been able to break in.

But some of David's soldiers found a small tunnel. It brought part of the city's water supply. It was cut through the rock from a spring outside. The soldiers climbed up the tunnel and then opened the gates of Jerusalem. Now the Hebrews had their city.

At that time, Jerusalem wasn't very big—about the size of two of our city blocks. Most streets were so narrow that two people couldn't walk side by side. But the city meant a lot to

the Hebrews. It wasn't just a center of government. It was also the center of their religion.

King David brought the Holy Ark into Jerusalem. The Ark was a large wooden box. Inside it were two stones with words on them. These words were the Ten Commandments.

Before the Hebrews took Jerusalem, they had carried the Ark with them from place to place. They kept it in a tent made of goatskins. Now David wanted to give the Ark a proper home. He planned to build a temple for it.

But David never did get around to building the temple. He was too busy with other jobs. He had to keep fighting

93

off attacks from the neighboring peoples. And he had to get the different Hebrew tribes to work together as a team.

When David died, his son Solomon became king. By this time, the Hebrews' way of life had begun to change. They had a country of their own. Most had stopped wandering and settled down. Solomon planned even bigger changes. He wanted Israel to be a rich and strong nation like Egypt.

King Solomon built a fabulous temple for the Ark. He also built an even more fabulous palace for himself. He improved the nation's defenses. The Hebrew army now had weapons made of iron. (Before, their weapons had been made of bronze, which bends easily.) The army also had chariots (CHAR-ee-uts) pulled by horses — the "tanks" of ancient times.

But some Hebrews did not like what Solomon was doing. To pay for all the changes, he made his people pay high taxes. To construct the new buildings, he forced many of the people to work like slaves. Some Hebrews said that Solomon was copying too many foreign ways. They said he was forgetting the simple beliefs of his own people. These feelings caused trouble when Solomon died. The Hebrew tribes could not agree on another king and split up again.

Yet Solomon is remembered as a wise king. Today, people are sometimes said to be "as wise as Solomon." He kept Israel at peace for 40 years. And, for the Jews who came afterward, he did something important. He built the temple.

Jerusalem was David's city. Solomon crowned it with the temple. Today, the ruins of David's city lie buried deep under the ground of the modern city. But for Jews, the ancient city still remains standing in their hearts. It marks the time and the place where they came together as a great nation.

By the time of King Solomon, the Hebrews were using chariots drawn by horses and mules. The Hebrews put chariots to work in farming and war.

You Be the Judge

King Solomon's wisdom was often called upon to solve daily problems among the Hebrew people. Here is a modern situation that would tax the wisdom of Solomon. You be the judge:

Jane Williams was only 17 when her son was born. Her husband drank a lot. He used to steal things from their own house to get money for liquor. Finally, she threw him out. But Jane couldn't find a job. Her whole world seemed to be caving in on her. She suffered a nervous breakdown. Her son, Russell, had to be placed in a foster home. When she got out of the hospital, Jane decided to give Russell up for adoption.

Russell was adopted by a well-to-do couple named Morrison. They gave him all the love and material things he could want. Russell developed into a happy and loving child.

Things went well for Jane Williams too. Shortly after she came out of the hospital she got a good job. Within two years, she had re-married. She and her new husband wanted a family of their own. But a year went by and Jane found she couldn't have another child. She now decided she wanted her first-born son, Russell, back. She and her husband sued the state to have Russell returned to them.

Russell's adopted parents were worried. They loved him dearly. He loved them too. He didn't remember Jane as his mother. The Morrisons said Russell would suffer terrible mental harm if he were taken away from them. Jane maintained that she loved Russell and that the child was rightfully hers.

Would you return Russell to his real mother or would you leave him in his adopted home?

5

"A Light to the Nations"

After Solomon's death, the Hebrews split up. The 10 northern tribes formed the Kingdom of Israel. This kingdom was always at war with its neighbors or facing revolts by its own people. In the south, the Kingdom of Judah didn't have as much trouble. But in the sixth century B.C. it faced a powerful enemy, the armies of Babylonia.

The year: 587 B.C.

The place: Jerusalem, capital of the small Hebrew kingdom of Judah.

The action: The city is surrounded by the armies of Babylonia.

Babylonian soldiers are pounding the walls of the city with heavy wooden logs. Inside the city, there is little food. People are dying of hunger. Some fall dead in the streets. The city cannot hold out much longer.

Why were the armies of Babylonia attacking the Hebrews? At this time, Babylonia was the strongest power in the area. Its king, Nebuchadnezzar (neh-boo-kad-NEH-zar), had forced Judah to become part of his empire. But the Hebrews hated their Babylonian masters. In 589 B.C. they rebelled. They hoped to get help from the pharaoh of Egypt.

*In 587 B.C. Babylonian armies stormed Jerusalem
and took many Hebrew prisoners. The Sumerian
wall carving at left gives an idea of how the
siege of Jerusalem might have looked. The carving
above shows Hebrews being forced into exile.*

Nebuchadnezzar quickly sent his army to surround
Jerusalem. The Babylonians were able to drive back an
Egyptian army that marched against them. Now Jerusalem
was doomed. The Babylonians broke open its wall and poured
into the city. The Hebrew king, Zedekiah (zeh-DEE-kee-uh),
tried to run away, but he was captured.

Nebuchadnezzar showed no mercy to the Hebrew king.
Zedekiah was forced to watch his own sons put to death.
Then he was blinded, put in chains, and taken to Babylon.
The Babylonians destroyed the Temple of Solomon, the
Hebrew house of worship. Then they burned down the city
and carried off many of its people to Babylonia.

The Hebrews were not treated badly in Babylonia. Many
were skilled workers, and the Babylonians found them useful.

They were allowed to move around freely and work at their trades or businesses. Yet some of them were not happy in Babylonia. They wished to return to their own "promised land." One of their poems tells of this feeling:

> By the waters of Babylon,
>> there we sat down and wept,
>> when we remembered Jerusalem.

The Hebrews wondered how they could worship God in a strange land that had many gods. They had no temple in Babylon, but could they not pray to God anyway? Wasn't God everywhere? In Babylon, the Hebrews renewed their faith, the faith given to them by Moses. Many had strayed from that faith and had worshiped gods of nature. Now they again saw themselves as the servants of the One True God. It was their purpose to bring the Word of God to others, to be "a light to the nations."

What finally happened to the Hebrews from Judah, or Jews? In 439 B.C., the Persian king, Cyrus, defeated Babylonia and made it part of his empire. Cyrus was a wise and kind ruler. He allowed the Jews in Babylon to return to their homeland, and many did so. He told them to rebuild the Temple of Solomon in Jerusalem, and gave them money to pay for it.

The Jewish state lasted until 63 B.C., when it was conquered by the Romans. The Jews often revolted to try to free themselves. Some of the revolts were at first successful. But the Romans always won.

In 70 A.D., the Romans destroyed Jerusalem and the temple. In the years that followed, many Jews left their homeland. They settled throughout the Roman Empire and the Middle East.

In their new homelands, Jews played important roles in the arts, the sciences, medicine, trade, and banking. Yet they had no nation to call their own. They did not, in fact, obtain one until the middle of this century. Then, in 1948, the nation of Israel was born.

Front Page

The headlines below could have appeared in a Phoenician or Hebrew newspaper—if these ancient people had ever had newspapers. Your job is to arrange the headlines below in proper order on another sheet. Put the event that happened first at the top, and so on. Then, for each headline, write a one-paragraph "news story." The story should tell what happened and why the event was important.

HEBREWS LEAVE BABYLON FOR JUDAH, SAY: THERE'S NO PLACE LIKE HOME

HEBREWS ESCAPE FROM SLAVERY IN EGYPT; MOSES HONORED AS GREAT LEADER

Solomon's Temple Built in Jerusalem; Hebrews Pleased with Their New Capital

Ten Commandments Accepted by Hebrews; Officials Predict a Period Of Law and Order

Phoenician Ship Lands on African Coast; Captain Says: "I Thank My Lucky Stars"

Part 3

Ancient Greece

Introduction: Through Greek Eyes

"The world is full of wonders, but nothing is more wonderful than man."

A Greek writer said this in the fifth century B.C. In one sentence, he summed up the most important beliefs of almost all Greeks:

Humans were something special;
they were worthy of honor and respect;
they were worthy of being free.

What made humans more wonderful than anything else the gods had made? A Greek would say: Only humans can build cities, create works of art, and develop sciences. They alone have the intelligence to guide their own lives and to know right from wrong.

Ideas such as these were very unusual in the world outside of Greece. In the Middle East and Egypt, people still bowed down to god-kings. The people never asked questions of their rulers.

The Greeks thought that such people were not much better than slaves. They believed that people could think and act for themselves. They could rule themselves better than any king could do. From these ideas came the idea of *democracy*, a Greek word meaning "rule by the people." The Greeks too had once had kings. But by the fifth century B.C., most Greeks lived in small city-states in which free men ruled themselves. These city-states had the world's first democratic governments.

The Greeks were first in many other things which are important to us today. They were the first to:

write plays and act in them,
write about history, and
develop many sciences.

Greek arts, sciences, and philosophy (ways of looking at life) later spread over much of the world. Today many of our ideas about politics, law, our rights and duties come from the Greeks.

Below, scholars go about their studies in a Greek classroom. Page 102: A musician strums a lyre to accompany his songs and recitations.

Ancient Greece (About 450 B.C.)

Ancient Greek civilization was centered on the mountainous Balkan peninsula south of Macedonia (above). The distance from Mt. Olympus in the north to Sparta in the south was less than 250 miles. Do you see a connection between Greek geography and the fact that the Greeks developed the world's first democracy? If so, how do you explain the connection?

Marking Time

B.C.

1600__	Greek civilization starts
1200__	Dorians conquer early Greeks
900__	Greek city-states develop
776__	First Olympic games held
650__	Rise of Athens
490__	Greeks defeat Persians at Marathon
479__	Persians defeat Spartans at Thermopylae
431__	Greeks defeat Persians at Salamis
404__	Wars between Sparta and Athens
338__	Philip of Macedonia conquers Greece
334__	Alexander defeats Persia, spreads Greek culture

B.C

- Greek civilization arose about 1600 B.C. How long ago was that?
- Approximately how many years did it take for Greek city-states to develop after the Dorian conquest?
- Which occurred first: the Greek victory at Salamis or Marathon?
- True or false? The first Olympic games took place in the eighth century B.C.

1

Athens: A Way of Life

Greece had hundreds of city-states, but two became stronger and greater than the others. They were Athens and Sparta. These city-states had very different life-styles. Athens became a great democracy, ruled by all its free men. (Women were not citizens.) Sparta became a soldier-state, ruled by a small group of men. The wealth of Athens came from its trade and colonies. Sparta's wealth came from land worked by slaves.

The year: about 450 B.C.
The place: a busy street in Athens.
The action: Two citizens, Ariston (AH-ruh-ston) and Cleros (KLAIR-ohz), are walking to the marketplace.

ARISTON: It looks like another fine sunny day, Cleros. There's not a cloud in the sky. And the sea breeze is as cool as ever.

CLEROS: What did you expect, Ariston? Who but the Greeks are blessed with such a climate? It keeps us outdoors and makes us healthy too.

(Suddenly a boy throws a pail of garbage into the street, shouting, "Out of the way.")

ARISTON: That fool slave boy! Why doesn't he watch where he throws the garbage? He almost hit me!

CLEROS: He's just a stupid barbarian. Don't expect *him* to have any sense.

ARISTON: Say, it's getting crowded. The marketplace will be busier than ever today. If only people wouldn't push and shove!

CLEROS: If you want to enjoy city life, Ariston, you have to put up with such things.

(The two men enter the marketplace. It is a large, open square filled with wooden booths. From these booths, merchants shout, "Fresh bread for sale!" "Buy fish!" "Olive oil today—get it today—get it cheap!" Around the square are long covered walks and temples to the gods.)

ARISTON: Cleros, do you see what I see? Isn't that the wife of Paros [PAH-roz] buying flowers?

CLEROS: Shocking! No decent woman should be seen in public! And here, among the rabble of the marketplace! She must have sneaked out of her house. Wait till Paros hears about this!

(A group of men are talking about the news of the day. ARISTON stops to listen to them for a while. Then he rejoins CLEROS.)

CLEROS: What are they saying?

ARISTON: Good news! Our fleet has won a great victory over the Persians at Cyprus [SY-press]! Perhaps now the king of Persia will leave our colonies in Asia alone. When will he learn that Persian barbarians can never defeat free Greeks?

CLEROS: Barbarians are slow to learn, Ariston. That is why we must keep our fleet strong at all times.

ARISTON: By the way, Cleros, is it true what people are saying about our noble leader, Pericles [PER-uh-cleez]? Does he really want to *pay* citizens to serve on juries?

CLEROS: Why, yes, Ariston. Does that bother you?

ARISTON: Really, Cleros, you surprise me. You know as well as I do that a man's first duty is to serve his city. The highest reward that any man could want is to take part in his government. Why should anyone have to be paid money for it?

CLEROS: Let's be practical, Ariston. How many men can afford to leave their jobs or farms to serve the city? We have about 30,000 citizens in Athens. Every one of them is supposed to vote in the assembly on new laws. Yet how many of them actually do vote in the assembly? Usually no more than 6,000. And the reason for it is that most citizens can't afford the time to go to meetings. I think Pericles has the right idea. If we pay our citizens to take part in running the government, more will be able to serve. It will make Athens even more democratic than it is now.

ARISTON: Perhaps you are right, Cleros. I never thought of it that way. Say, what are you doing this afternoon?

CLEROS: I think I'll go to my gymnasium, Ariston. A man must have a healthy body as well as an educated mind. Besides, I hear Euripides [you-RIP-uh-deez] will be there. He's written a play, and I want to know about it.

ARISTON: I would like to meet this new writer. Do you mind if I come along with you?

CLEROS: Not at all. See you at the gym after lunch.

Ancient Greek drama grew out of earlier rituals such as the one being performed by the woman at left.

What If. . . ?

If the Greek Ariston came to your community, what would he think of it? What answers do you think Ariston would give to these questions about your community?

■ How democratic is the government? Do all citizens vote *directly* for laws? Do all government workers serve because it is their duty?

■ Are most people in good physical shape or are they flabby? Do they spend time every day improving their minds and their bodies?

■ What would Ariston think about the roles of modern women?

■ Is this community clean and prosperous? In Athens "flying garbage" was a problem. Are there similar problems here?

2
Sparta: A Way of Life

Stranger, tell the Spartans that we lie here obedient to their laws.

These words were written on the grave of 300 Spartan soldiers. They had fought to the last man against a large army of Persians at Thermopylae (thur-MAHP-eh-lee) in 480 B.C. Before the battle, they were told that the arrows of the Persians would fly in such numbers they would hide the sun. A Spartan soldier said: "So much the better. We shall fight in the shade."

Spartan soldiers were the best in Greece, and they were very brave. They did not give up or run. They fought until they won—or died. Spartan fighters were trained to be that way from the time they were born. They were taught to become good soldiers and obey their leaders. They were not allowed to have any trade or job. That was for slaves. Spartan men had to be soldiers, and nothing else.

Why did Sparta raise its boys to become professional soldiers? Like other Greek city-states, Sparta did not have enough land to feed its people. Other city-states solved the problem by sending their "extra" people to overseas colonies.

Sparta solved the problem another way: It made war on its neighbor, Messenia (meh-SEE-nee-uh). Sparta took over the land of Messenia and made slaves of the people. The number of slaves in the area Sparta now ruled was much larger than the number of Spartans. There were about 10 slaves for every Spartan citizen.

About 650 B.C., the slaves rebelled against their Spartan masters. It took the Spartans almost 20 years to put down the slaves. After that the Spartans lived in fear of other slave rebellions. They decided that they should have a strong army ready at all times. So the Spartans were trained to become tough soldiers and obey orders. They spent almost all their time building their bodies. Spartan girls also had to have strong, healthy bodies. The Spartans cared very little about improving their minds. Usually they looked down on learning any new ideas.

This is how Agis (AY-jess), a Spartan boy, was trained:

Soon after Agis was born, a group of Spartan leaders looked him over. They saw that he was a healthy baby and gave him back to his parents. Agis was lucky. Sick or weak Spartan babies were thrown into a deep hole to die.

Agis had nurses who did not spoil him. They taught him to be content with very plain food. They taught him not to fear the dark and never to cry.

At the age of seven, Agis had to leave home and live in a camp with the other young boys. He slept on a hard bed and wore few clothes, even in cold weather. He was taught by a trainer:

to stand pain,
to speak only when he was spoken to,
to answer in a few words,
to respect his elders without question,
to obey every order completely,
to harden his body, and
to eat very little.

When Agis became a teenager, he was sometimes sent to live alone in the woods. He was given no food. He had to find food, or steal it. If he didn't, he would starve. If caught, he would be whipped. This was to train the future soldier to take care of himself.

Agis and the other boys in his camp played rough games. In one game, two teams of 15 players each fought to keep a ball. There were no rules. Biting, punching, and kicking were allowed. The winning team was the one that had the ball when "time" was called. In another game, two teams fought each other on an island in a river. The team that pushed the other into the river won.

Spartan sports were not always so rough. Agis was taught to drill and exercise with music playing. Agis liked that. He and the other boys were taught to read and write. But they had very little use for books.

At 18, Agis reached manhood. He trained with the army and was allowed to let his hair grow long. Spartans believed that long hair was a sign of manliness. They liked to curl it and adorn it too. At 24, Agis became a first-class soldier. At 30, he became a full citizen. He was now allowed to live at home with his wife and young children. It was the first time since he was a small boy that he had lived in a real home.

Even so, Agis had to eat dinner every day with other soldiers rather than with his family. When war came, he had to put on his armor and march off. He had to serve in the army until he was 60.

It was better for Agis not to give up or run away in a battle. The Spartans were rough on "cowards." Soldiers who quit in a battle lost all their rights. Other Spartans would have nothing to do with them or their families. Spartan women had the same spirit. When a Spartan soldier went to war, his mother told him: "Come back with your shield, or on it."

Who Said That?

The quotes below might have been said by a citizen of either Sparta or Athens. Basing your views on the information in this chapter, decide which Greek probably made the statement.

- **Mother to son going off to war:** "If you can't come back a winner, don't come back at all."

- **Teacher to students:** "Every day we'll do word exercises to sharpen your mind, and physical exercises to tone up your body."

- **Teacher to students:** "Shoes soften your feet. The rule here is everyone goes barefoot at all times."

- **Soldier to wife:** "Now that I'm 60, I'm finally able to retire from the army."

- **Citizen to friend:** "Don't you agree, it's the responsibility of all citizens to serve on juries?"

- **Government leader to his assistant:** "This baby is a weakling. He will be a burden to the state. Throw him into that hole."

3

Heroes of Marathon

King Darius (duh-RYE-us) of Persia wanted to punish Athens. He knew how to do it. He would burn the city to the ground and make slaves of its people. Then he would send them away to a distant part of his vast empire.

Why was Darius so angry with Athens? The king of Persia was a proud man. He was the master of a great empire that reached from India to Egypt. In this empire, everyone had to bow to the "Great King." They had to pay him tribute (taxes) and provide soldiers to serve in his armies. They were ruled by his governors.

But in 499 B.C. Greek colonies in Asia Minor (modern Turkey) rebelled against Persian rule. They asked Athens to help. Athens sent 20 warships to Asia Minor. These ships helped the rebels burn a Persian city. Later the Persians put down the rebellion. But Darius never forgave Athens for aiding it.

In 492 B.C. Darius sent a large fleet with soldiers to punish Athens. He now meant to add all of Greece to his empire. This fleet was wrecked at sea by a storm. But two years later Darius sent another fleet of 600 ships to Athens. This time the fleet put the Persian army ashore at Marathon, only 22 miles from Athens. There the Persian army of about 25,000 men set up camp.

At Marathon, the Athenians met a powerful enemy,
King Darius of Persia. In this piece of
sculpture, he is shown seated on his throne.

The citizens of Athens voted to send an army to Marathon at once. About 10,000 men were able to answer the call to arms. They went home, put on their armor, took their weapons, and marched off. The Athenian army set up camp on a mountain one mile from the Persians.

Now the 10 generals of Athens wondered what to do. They could see that the Persian army was much larger than their own. The Persians also had horse soldiers and men with bows and arrows. The Athenians had neither. Some of the Athenian generals were against attacking the Persians. It would be safer to stay where they were. Besides, the Spartans had promised to send help in a few days. It would be better to wait for the Spartans to arrive before fighting the Persians.

Other generals wanted to attack the Persians quickly. One of them, Miltiades (mil-TIE-ah-deez), had good reasons for it: He feared that traitors inside Athens might try to make a deal with the Persians. He believed that free Greek citizens fighting for their homes could defeat the Persian "slaves."

The generals finally agreed to support Miltiades. He became the leader of the Athenian army. Miltiades ordered the Athenians to attack on the run. He wanted to close the space between the two armies quickly. He believed that in close fighting the Greeks would have many advantages. The Greeks wore body armor; the Persians did not. Greek shields were made of metal and hides; Persian shields were made of twigs. Greek spears were longer than Persian spears.

The Persians were amazed when they saw the Athenians running toward them. They thought the Athenians were madmen, rushing to get killed.

But soon the Greeks' weapons and style of fighting were too much for the Persians. Early in the battle the Persians broke through the center of the Greeks' line. But the Greek wings wheeled around and formed a line *behind* the Persians. The Persians fought bravely. But solid rows of Greek shields and long spears were too much for them. Finally, the Persians

118

ran back to their ships. The Greeks chased them and captured seven of their ships. The rest of the Persian fleet put to sea.

Miltiades sent a runner to Athens, more than 25 miles away, with news of the victory. But the Persian commander had a trick up his sleeve. He ordered his fleet to sail to Athens. He hoped the city would be without guards to defend it. Then traitors might turn the city over to him. But Miltiades guessed the Persian commander's plan. He marched most of his army overland to Athens. When the Persian fleet arrived, its commander could see the Athenian soldiers ready and waiting. The Persians knew their cause was hopeless. They sailed back to Asia.

The next day a Spartan army arrived at Marathon. The army saw the dead on the battlefield. There were 6,400 Persians and 192 Athenians. The Athenian heroes were buried in a mound that can still be seen today.

The Athenian victory at Marathon did not stop the Persians from attacking Greece again. But it did show the other city-states that the Persians could be beaten. It gave some Greeks the will to resist and even to unite against the Persians. In 480 B.C. the Greeks united against the next Persian attack. The Persian army defeated a small Spartan army at a mountain pass called Thermopylae (see page 111). Every Spartan was killed defending the mountain pass. Then the Persians took Athens and burned its temples.

But soon after, the Greek fleet almost wiped out a larger Persian fleet. This crushing defeat forced most of the Persian army to go home. The rest of the Persians were driven from Greece for good the next year. It meant that Greek ideas of freedom and the worth of man would not die.

The defeat of the Persians filled all Greeks with pride, but especially the Athenians. They would never forget their heroes. The Athenians gained a great confidence in their own abilities. A "Golden Age" was about to begin for Athens in politics, trade, the arts and sciences.

Mapping the Wars

⊗ Battle Sites
•••••• Route of Persian Navy 480 B.C.
——— Route of Persian Army 480 B.C.

Scale of Miles

0   50   100   150

- Name three battles of the Persian wars.

- Miltiades sent a runner from Marathon to Athens to announce his victory over the Persians. In which direction did the runner have to travel? Today we use the word *marathon* to refer to a long-distance race. About how many miles did this runner have to travel?

- What body of water is located to the east of the Greek city-states?

- Which sea did the Persian navy sail through to reach Salamis? Why do you think the ships stayed so close to the shore?

4
The Golden Age

*It was the liveliest city in all of Greece. People rushed to see
great plays in large outdoor theaters. On a high hill, artists
were building new temples and statues of the gods. In busy streets,
men argued about the meaning of justice, truth, and goodness.
In gymnasiums they boxed, wrestled, and trained their bodies.
Thousands of them met almost every week to hear their leaders
and make new laws.*

*This was Athens, Greece, during its Golden Age. It began
about 479 B.C. after the defeat of the Persians. Athens was then
the richest and strongest Greek city-state. Its great wealth gave
many men free time to serve their city and enjoy "the good life."*

How did Athens become so rich and strong? No one had
done more than the Athenians to save Greece from the
Persians. When the Persians were defeated in 479 B.C., Athens
had a very powerful navy. Now Athens asked other Greek
city-states to join it in a league.

Athens offered to protect them against the Persians. They,
in return, would pay Athens either in ships or money. Many
city-states thought this was a good idea and joined the
league. Athens grew rich and powerful as its leader.

*An Ionic column from an ancient Athenian temple
rises into the sky. Such structures as this remain
lasting examples of the "glory that was Greece."*

During its Golden Age, Athens had many great writers, artists, and wise men. The wisest of all was a short, fat, homely man who was too poor to buy shoes. His name was Socrates (SOCK-rah-teez). Everyone in Athens knew him.

He could always be found, either in the streets, the marketplace, or a gym; and he was always talking. Mostly he liked to ask questions, lots of questions. What, he asked men, was the meaning of truth? Of goodness? Of right or wrong? Of justice? His questions often made men angry.

Socrates wanted Athenians to think for themselves. He wanted them to look for the truth and not accept what other people *said* was true.

Socrates asked many questions, but he rarely gave answers. He believed that the wisest men were those who admitted that they knew very little. Only the gods were really wise. Men who boasted that they were wise were just fools.

Socrates loved to show these "wise" men how foolish they were. He would ask them questions that seemed very simple at first. But soon he would set a trap for them. Then their answers would become nonsense, and they would feel very stupid. This is how Socrates would question a man who thought he was very wise:

SOCRATES: Tell me, if you can, what is courage?

MAN: Easy. A man has courage if he fights against the enemy and does not run away.

SOCRATES: Very well. Then courage is something very noble. Is that true?

MAN: Very true.

SOCRATES: Suppose a man does not run away when the enemy is sure to kill him. What would you call that?

MAN: I would call that very foolish.

SOCRATES: But isn't it also courage?

MAN: Well . . . I suppose so.

SOCRATES: Then you are saying that courage is both noble and foolish? How can that be?

Socrates died as he lived, asking questions in the search for truth. This famous 18th-century painting by Jacques Louis David shows Socrates on his deathbed.

MAN: I don't know. You've got me all mixed up. I don't know what I'm saying anymore.

During its Golden Age, Athens respected a man like Socrates. His questions often disturbed people, but most agreed he was the wisest man among them. But the Golden Age ended after Athens went to war with Sparta (see page 132). Hard times and disorder came to the city. Many people then believed that Socrates was a dangerous troublemaker. Because of him, they said, men were not loyal to the city or the gods. Socrates was put on trial for "not worshiping the gods and for corrupting the young men of the city."

Socrates refused to save his life by saying he was wrong and asking for mercy. Instead he boldly defended himself. His only crime, he said, was searching for truth and wisdom. The gods themselves had commanded him to do so, he told the jury.

Socrates was found guilty. He was sentenced to death by drinking poison. His friends were with him in jail when he calmly drank the cup of poison. Until the very end, he asked them questions.

What Would You Have Said?

If you met Socrates, he might ask you lots of questions. On a separate sheet of paper, write down the answers you would give him. Try to include a specific example in your reply. A possible answer for number one has been given. Do you agree with it? Is there only one "right" answer to each of Socrates' questions?

If Socrates asked:	You would answer:
1 What is GOODNESS?	*(Goodness is being considerate of other people. A good person will try to cheer up a friend who is feeling low.)*
2 What is TRUTH?	
3 What is JUSTICE?	
4 What is COURAGE?	
5 What is BEAUTY?	

5

The Olympic Games

Most Greeks wanted their men to be all-around men. They believed in developing their minds and their muscles. The best kind of Greek was both a thinker and an athlete. (Only boys went to school. Girls were taught at home.)

An important building in each city was the gymnasium. Physical training played a big part in the schools. Boys of high school age practiced running and jumping. They learned to swim, wrestle, and throw a javelin. They took "driver ed" in horse-drawn chariots.

Every four years, a big contest was held in a place called Olympia (uh-LIM-pee-uh). People came there from all over Greece and its colonies. These Olympic games were more than a sporting event. They were also a religious festival. They were an offering to the god Zeus (zooss).

The first known games were held in 776 B.C. They became so important that Greeks numbered the years from that date. The ancient games died out after the Romans took over Greece. But they gave us the idea for today's Olympic games.

What do you suppose the ancient games might have been like if the Greeks had had radio? Let's go back to the fifth century B.C. and find out. Now to our man at the stadium. Come in, Damon (DAY-mon). . . .

DAMON: And it's a most exciting moment! The 200-yard dash is about to begin. This is one of the five events known as the pentathlon [pen-TATH-lon]. If any man wins three of these events, he's the winner of the pentathlon.

Cleon [KLEE-on] of Athens has already won two events. He was top man in the discus and the javelin. Zeno [ZEE-no] of Sparta just beat him in the broad jump. And Zeno is expected to win the wrestling. He's bigger and heavier than Cleon. So it all depends on the 200-yard dash.

JASON: There's a big crowd here this afternoon. It's a hot summer day. There are trees on the hills all around. But there's no shade here in the stadium. We sit on bleachers made of dried earth. It's terribly hot. The wine and fruit sellers are doing a lot of business.

We're still waiting for the athletes to come in. People are looking at the entrance, over by the temple buildings. By the way, there's a new statue in the main temple. It's of Zeus sitting on a throne. It's 60 feet high and covered with gold. Some people think it's too showy. They made a joke about it. They asked what would happen to the roof if Zeus stood up. But most people think it's wonderful. Over to you, Damon.

DAMON: Can you hear the crowd roaring? The contestants are coming in. Yes, there's Cleon . . . and Zeno. They've had themselves rubbed down with olive oil. Their bodies are shining like metal in the sunlight. Now they're lining up at the end of the track.

And they're off! The white sand is spurting up from their bare feet! It's Cleon in the lead! All the Athenians in the crowd are cheering like crazy. A lot of people are 'ooking glum. They must be Spartans.

Yes, Cleon has a two-yard lead over Zeno. They're nearly at the finish rocks. And now it's over. Cleon crossed the finish rocks first! He's won the pentathlon too!

The only prize he'll get here is a crown made of olive

leaves. But the people back home in Athens will make a big fuss over him. Maybe they'll give him a free dinner every day for the rest of his life. That's what a lot of cities give their big winners. They may put up a statue of him too. Or get someone to write a song about him. And now, over to Jason, who has an interesting interview.

JASON: It'll be some time before the wrestling begins. But don't go away. There are two spectators here who are arguing about the games. Let's see what they have to say. Excuse me, sir. What is your name?

SCOPAS: I'm Scopas [SKO-pas] from Corinth [KAR-anth]. And I think the games are going to pot. Most of the athletes these days aren't all-around men. They're professionals. They spend all their time training for the games. They're no good at anything else.

JASON: And you, sir?

MILO: I'm Milo [MY-low] from Athens. It's true, a lot of the athletes *are* professionals. But I still think the games are great. They bring all Greeks together. Look, Athens isn't on good terms with Corinth or Sparta. But we forget our quarrels while the games are on. It wouldn't even matter if Athens and Sparta were at war. I could still travel through Sparta to get to the games. No one would attack me.

SCOPAS: I still say the games aren't what they used to be. They're getting worse all the time.

MILO: Maybe. But they're too important to be forgotten. People will still remember them thousands of years in the future.

JASON: Well, I don't know about that. The games have been going strong for more than 300 years. But we can only guess at the future.

And now the crowd is roaring again. Yes, the wrestling matches are about to begin! . . .

Playing the Game

In this chapter, the Greek Scopas complained that the Olympic games were becoming "too professional." Today the Olympic games are supposed to be for amateur athletes only. But there is much criticism. The cartoon below offers an opinion of the modern Olympic games.

FORWARD TO THE NEXT GAMES!

- What is the purpose of the Olympic games?

- What does the cartoonist seem to feel about the games? Do you agree with him?

- Do you think the Olympic games can bring people of many nations closer? Or do they cause more problems than they are worth?

6

The Greeks
Defeat Themselves

The people of Athens were angry. Only six miles away, Spartan soldiers were ruining the Athenians' farmlands. Olive trees, grape vines, and corn fields were destroyed. The young men of Athens wanted to fight the Spartans. But Pericles, the leader of Athens, told them to stay inside the city walls. He knew that the Spartan army was too strong for Athens. However, Athens' navy was second to none, and the city was rich. Pericles was sure that ships and money would defeat the Spartans. Soon the warships of Athens were raiding towns on the coast of Sparta.

So began the war between Athens and Sparta in 431 B.C. — a war that *had* to come, people said. For many years, some Greeks had feared that Athens was getting too big, too strong, and too bossy. In 479 B.C. Athens had started a league of Greek city-states to guard against Persia (see page 122). At first Athens was its leader. But soon Athens became its "boss." City-states were not allowed to quit the league. If they tried to quit, they were put down by force. They had to pay money to Athens, whether they liked it or not. The league really became Athens' empire.

Other Greek city-states were jealous of Athens' power. They feared that Athens might try to take over *all* Greece. Sparta was especially worried by Athens. Finally, in 431 B.C., Sparta voted to go to war against Athens. Both Athens and Sparta had many allies among the city-states. The allies came into the war too. The war lasted almost 30 years and was very hard. Little mercy was shown by either side. Many innocent people were killed as Greeks fought Greeks.

Athens' suffering was very great. The farmers who grew food for Athens had to move inside the city walls when the war began. The city became very crowded. Most of the farmers had to sleep in the streets, in temples, or in huts.

The people of Athens blamed Pericles for all their troubles. They wanted to make peace with Sparta. They said that Pericles had dragged them into the war. They shook their fists at him and cursed him.

Pericles gave them his answer in a speech. He reminded them of their duty to defend Athens. If the city fell, he said, they would all be ruined. Then he reminded them that they too had voted for the war. He accused them of being weak and not able to take setbacks. Finally, he reminded them that they had a great empire. "Half the world is yours—the sea," he said. The people of Athens must defend that empire or become slaves. Pericles told them to be worthy of their past glory.

The Athenians were won over by Pericles' speech. They agreed to go on with the war against Sparta. But a year later, in 429 B.C., Pericles died. He died of an awful sickness that spread over the city. About one person in every four died. Dead bodies were piled up in the streets.

The war went on for many years. Sometimes Athens seemed to be winning; at other times Sparta seemed to be winning. Finally, in 404 B.C., Athens had to surrender. The walls of the city were torn down. Athens now had to obey cruel rulers chosen by the Spartans. The Golden Age of Athens was over.

Puzzling It Out

In this puzzle you have to find both the answer and the question.

1 W	2	3	4

5	6 A	7

8	9	10	11	12	13 L	14	15

16	17 E	18	19	20	21	22

23	24	25

| 26 | 27 | 28 H | 29 | 30 | 31 |
|---|---|---|---|---|---| **?**

Here's how it works. Copy the diagram onto a separate sheet of paper. The boxes in the top part, when filled in, will contain the question. The answer to that question is in white circles which run down the bottom part of the puzzle.

It's a good idea to start with the bottom of the puzzle. Fill in the answers to the definitions in the spaces at the right. Notice that every box at the top has a number. Every circle at the bottom also has a number. Take the letters at the bottom and put them in the boxes at the top which have the same number. We've done one of the definitions to help give you a start.

A. One place to keep money or jewels; means the same as secure.

B. A short form of sister.

C. To get together; rhymes with rather.

D. A huge sea mammal.

E. An agreement; rhymes with fact.

F. A rolling stone gathers no _____.

G. More recent; rhymes with sewer.

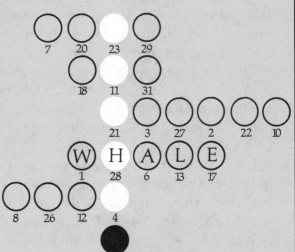

7

Alexander the Great

The long, bloody war between Athens and Sparta left the city-states of Greece without strength. Even Sparta was too weak to control Greece for long. Other city-states rose against Sparta. In 371 B.C. Sparta was defeated by Thebes (theebz). It was never again a great power.

The real winner of the wars among the Greeks was an outsider. King Philip the Second of Macedonia (mas-uh-DOE-nee-uh), a land to the north, defeated the weakened cities of Greece. By 338 B.C. Philip was the supreme ruler of Greece.

King Philip of Macedonia was in a good mood. He was giving a great feast for his daughter's wedding. Many Greeks had come to honor him. There was music, dancing, games, and lots of food. Just as Philip was about to see some plays in a theater, an assassin pulled out a dagger. He stabbed Philip to death before guards could stop him.

The people in the theater started to panic. Then a handsome young man of 20 spoke to them from the stage. He told them to stay calm. "Nothing has changed," he said, "except the

In just 11 years a fearless young Macedonian, later called Alexander the Great, won himself an empire.

name of the king." The people cheered. Soldiers crowded around him. For this young man was Philip's son, Alexander, the next king of Macedonia. In a few years, he would defeat and rule Persia, the largest empire in the world. He would be called Alexander the Great.

What was this young king like? He had already shown that he was a good soldier. At 18 he had helped his father defeat Greek armies and had fought bravely. Yet no man admired the Greeks more than Alexander. The Greeks had given the world its greatest poets, writers, and thinkers. Alexander read all their books. He even slept with a book of Greek poetry under his pillow. His teacher was Aristotle (ah-ruh-STOT-el), the best thinker in all Greece. From Aristotle, Alexander learned Greek ideas of right and wrong, and politics.

Alexander knew what he wanted to do. Once the great empire of Persia had tried to defeat the Greeks. Now Alexander would lead the Macedonians and Greeks against Persia. He was sure he would win. Then he would set up new Greek cities all over the Persian Empire. He would make almost the whole world Greek, and he, Alexander, would rule it!

In the spring of 334 B.C., Alexander led his army of 40,000 men into Asia. He was then only 22 years old. His army carried heavy weapons of war. There were:

towers on wheels to attack high walls;
battering rams to break down walls;
large catapults, or slings, to throw heavy rocks;
small catapults that threw several spears at once.

The Persians were again led by a king named Darius. But the King Darius of Alexander's time was not as great a warrior as the earlier King Darius. Alexander's army met Darius' army in Asia Minor (modern Turkey). Alexander's horse soldiers broke the Persian lines, and Darius ran away. But Darius' mother, wife, and two daughters were taken prisoner.

Soon after, Darius wrote to Alexander. He asked Alexander

to return his family to him. He offered Alexander friendship in return. Alexander's answer was very rough. He said Darius would have to ask him in person for his family. And Darius would have to treat him as "Lord of all Asia." If not, Alexander wrote, "stand your ground and fight for it. Do not run away, for I will chase you any place you go."

Alexander did chase the Persian king and finally found him—dead. He had been murdered by one of his own men. Alexander had Darius buried in a royal tomb. But he showed no mercy to the man who had murdered his own king.

Alexander had won the largest empire in the world, but

The Empire of Alexander the Great

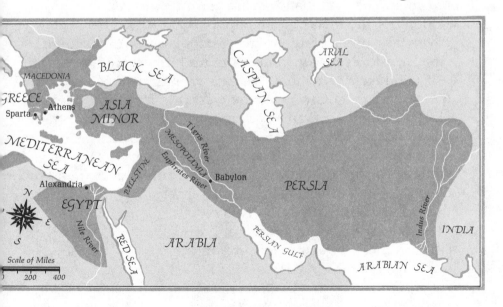

At his death in 323 B.C., Alexander's empire stretched from Greece into India. Which of these lands had once been ruled by other great civilizations already mentioned in this book?

could he hold it by force alone? Alexander knew it would be impossible. He had to win the friendship of the Persians to keep peace in his empire. Soon Alexander began to treat Persians as the equals of Greeks and Macedonians. He took many Persians into his army and his government. Alexander married a daughter of Darius and often wore Persian clothes. He had 10,000 of his soldiers marry Persian girls!

Many of Alexander's officers became angry with him. They thought he was being *too* friendly to the Persians. They refused to fight for him anymore and asked to go home. One of them told him:

"This, Alexander, is what hurts us: You have made Persians your kinsmen [relatives], and they are allowed to kiss you. But no Macedonian has this right."

Alexander answered quickly. "But all of you are my kinsmen," he said, "and from now on I will call you so."

Many of the Macedonians then kissed Alexander. Later he gave a feast to celebrate. At the feast thousands of Macedonians, Greeks, and Persians drank wine from the same bowls.

It had taken Alexander 11 years to win his great empire. It stretched from Greece in the west into India in the east. He had fought hard and had many wounds. He had often gone without food or water. In June 323 B.C., he was in the city of Babylon. He was planning to explore the coast of Arabia. But he suddenly became sick with a fever. In a few days, Alexander the Great was dead. The man who had "ruled the world" was not yet 33 years old.

Alexander the Great left behind him about 70 new Greek cities in the old Persian Empire. In these cities, Greek learning was preserved.

One of these cities, Alexandria in Egypt, became the leading center of trade and learning in the ancient world. But later Alexandria came under the rule of a great new empire led by Rome. The city of Rome passed Alexandria in wealth and power. Rome became the greatest city in the world.

Front Page

Your job is to arrange the headlines below in proper order on another sheet. Put the event that happened first at the top, and so on. Then, for each headline, write a one-paragraph "news story." The story should tell what happened and why the event was important.

**Greeks Defeat Persians
At Battle of Marathon;
Runner Brings News of
Victory to Athenians**

**Alexander Gives Party
For Greeks, Persians,
Macedonians; Says:
"You've Got a Friend in Me"**

**GREEKS DECLARE
HUMANS SPECIAL,
SAY "IT'S ALL
IN THE MIND"**

**Socrates Accused of
Too Much Questioning;
"What Are the Answers?"
Greeks Want To Know**

**PERICLES ADDRESSES CROWD,
ASKS "DOVES" TO CONTINUE
FIGHT AGAINST SPARTAN FOE**

Part 4

The Roman Republic

Introduction: The Spirit of Patriots

They were brave, they were tough, they were honest, and they were patriots. They farmed the land and defended it against all their enemies. They might lose battles, but they always came back stronger. The stories told about these people, the early Romans, still inspire us today. For these are stories of great courage, honor, and loyalty. Probably these stories are only partly true. But they tell us a lot about the Roman spirit. Here are two of them:

• An army of Etruscans (ee-TRUSS-kinz), enemies of Rome, was about to capture the city. The Etruscans had only to cross a narrow wooden bridge to enter the city. The Roman leader ordered his men to chop down the bridge. But until the bridge fell, someone had to hold back the Etruscans on the other side. A soldier named Horatius (huh-RAY-shuss) offered himself for this "impossible" mission. Horatius fought the Etruscans until the bridge fell into the river. He was wounded, but swam back safely to the shore. There the Roman people cheered him for saving the city. It was about 500 B.C.

Romans built their empire log by log and stone by stone. They did it with such skill that some of their early structures still stand. Page 142: What does this portrait of a man and wife from the city of Pompeii tell you about the people of the empire?

• A Roman general named Regulus (REG-you-lus) was taken prisoner in a war against Carthage (CAR-thij). Carthage sent Regulus back to Rome to ask the Romans to make peace. Regulus promised to return to Carthage as a prisoner if Rome said "no." In Rome, Regulus told the Senate not to make peace with Carthage. He asked them to fight on against the enemy. Then, true to his promise, he went back to Carthage. There he was tortured and put to death. The year was about 250 B.C.

Heroes like these helped ancient Rome to last a thousand years. The small city-state grew into the greatest empire in the ancient world. The Roman Empire was even larger than that of Alexander the Great. The Roman Empire took in all the land around the Mediterranean Sea and more. At the center of this Mediterranean empire was Italy and the city of Rome.

After a long time, the Roman Empire began to crack and finally fell apart. But it left many things that are still part of today's world:

• *Roman law:* Today, Roman ideas of justice are in force in many countries. The aim of law, a Roman emperor said, was "to live honestly, to injure no one, and to give every man his right."

• *The Latin language and writing:* The Romans spoke and wrote Latin. Many languages of today come from it. Spanish, Italian, and French are the main ones. Even many English words come from Latin. Roman writers and poets at first imitated the Greeks, whom they admired. Later the Romans wrote books and poems in their own style. Many of them are still read today.

• *Buildings, roads, and bridges:* The Romans were great builders and engineers. Some Roman roads and aqueducts (ACK-wuh-duktz; bridges for carrying water) are still used today. New buildings are made in the Roman style even now. Modern sports stadiums look very much like the Roman Coliseum (cahl-uh-SEE-uhm).

• *Peace and unity:* The Roman Empire united many different peoples and nations for a long time. While the empire was strong, people in it were not troubled by wars. They could travel and trade freely. Peace in the Western world disappeared when the Roman Empire fell.

Marking Time

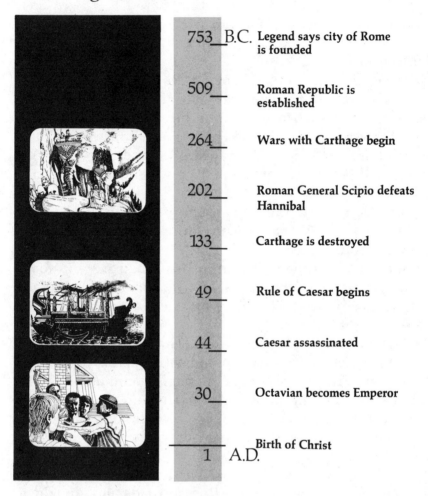

753 B.C.	**Legend says city of Rome is founded**
509	**Roman Republic is established**
264	**Wars with Carthage begin**
202	**Roman General Scipio defeats Hannibal**
133	**Carthage is destroyed**
49	**Rule of Caesar begins**
44	**Caesar assassinated**
30	**Octavian becomes Emperor**
1 A.D.	**Birth of Christ**

- Is the following statement true or false? The Roman Republic was established in the sixth century B.C.

- True or false? The destruction of Carthage took place more than a century before Caesar's rule began.

- A famous general from Carthage was defeated by a Roman army in the third century B.C. Who was he?

- The Roman Republic ended when the first emperor took power. How many years did the Republic last?

1

A Father's Choice

Rome began as a group of villages on the Tiber (TIE-bur) River. Some time in the eighth century B.C., *these villages became a town — Rome. At first it was ruled by Etruscan kings from north of Rome. But the Romans rebelled and freed themselves of Etruscan rule. This chapter tells of an incident in this war of freedom. Which value did Brutus place higher: loyalty to his city-state or protection of his children? Was his decision the right one?*

The young men were tied to wooden poles. Their clothes were ripped off and they were beaten with sticks. But the worst was still to come. For these young men were traitors to Rome. Their final punishment would be death.

All of these young men came from rich and noble families. Two of them were sons of Junius Brutus (JUNE-ee-uhz BROO-tuhz), the Roman consul (elected government leader). Brutus had the power to pardon these traitors. Would he do it? Or would he let his own sons die as an example to others? The Roman crowd watched Brutus closely. They knew how much he was suffering, and pitied him.

What was Brutus thinking at this moment? Did he think of Tarquin (TAR-kwin) the Proud, the former King of Rome? Brutus hated all that Tarquin stood for. Tarquin was no

Italy, Sixth Century B.C.

ALPS

Po River

Ravenna

Tiber River

CORSICA

ADRIATIC SEA

Rome

ITALY

SARDINIA

Neapolis

TYRRHENIAN SEA

N
W   E
S

IONIAN SEA

SICILY

Carthage

NORTH AFRICA

Scale of Miles
0   40   80   120

Area settled by the Etruscans

Roman. He was an outsider, an Etruscan. He and his kind had been in power too long.

Brutus hated Tarquin for his cruel one-man rule. Tarquin did not ask the Roman Senate for its advice. The Senate was a group of noble landowners who were called *patricians* (pah-TRISH-uhnz). Tarquin made war or peace without asking these Roman leaders for their opinion. He had put some Roman senators to death, and had taken the property of others.

Finally, in 509 B.C., Brutus swore that he would get rid of Tarquin. He stirred up a revolt. The angry people drove Tarquin and his sons out of Rome. Then the people elected Brutus and another man consuls. Rome became a republic. It would have no more kings.

But Tarquin did not give up easily. He knew that many young nobles did not like the Republic. Under the king, they had received special treatment. If they broke a law, the king often forgave them. But in the Republic, the law treated rich men and poor men as equals.

So Tarquin sent agents to some of these young nobles in Rome. And they promised to help Tarquin become king again. Two of them were the sons of Brutus. But the young nobles made a bad mistake. They wrote letters to Tarquin saying they would hand over Rome to him. A slave found these letters and showed them to Brutus. Brutus arrested all the young nobles and put them in prison. Later they were sentenced to die as traitors.

Brutus was in charge of carrying out the sentence. When the day came, everyone watched him. Would he let his own sons die?

Probably Brutus wished to forgive them. But his duty was to punish traitors. He hid his suffering. He did not blink while the traitors were beheaded.

Was Brutus a hard man? Perhaps. But the early Romans had to be tough. The small city-state was fighting for its life

149

against enemies who were all around the area. The early Romans were farmers who worked hard and lived simply. But when Rome was attacked, they quickly left their farms and became soldiers. Their courage and strong sense of duty made them good soldiers.

Romans first learned the importance of duty and loyalty as children at home. In the Roman family, the father had complete power. His wife and children had to obey him in everything. He arranged the marriages of his sons and daughters, and controlled their property. He had the right to kill a child who did not obey him. He also had the right to sell a child into slavery. Roman fathers did not use these rights often. But it was enough that they had them. Roman children learned early to obey and respect their fathers. Later their fathers taught them to have the same obedience and respect for Rome.

This wall sculpture charts a Roman boy's progress from playful babyhood to later boyhood. In the scene at right he recites lessons to his father. In what ways does Roman education seem similar to your own?

150

A Modern Father's Choice

GENERAL'S SON LEAVES COUNTRY

May 15: It was learned today that the son of retired Air Force General James Hunter has left for Canada as a war resister. Jim Hunter, Jr., has often taken an active part in antiwar demonstrations.

General Hunter was a key military planner in his day. In the past he has appealed to the public to support the war effort. He has gone on record as saying that all Americans must give total loyalty to the policies of their government.

The General could not be reached for comment about his son's behavior.

- How is General Hunter's story similar to that of Junius Brutus? In what ways do the two stories differ?

- If you were General Hunter, how would you feel about your son's trip?

- If you were asked whether your son should be punished, what would you say? Would you favor punishing your son for the good of the country? Or would you think your son had done the right thing? In either case, would your family ties change your views?

- What advice might the Roman father Brutus have given General Hunter? Do you think most American parents share the same values as Brutus? Do you think the ancient Romans showed themselves to be of strong character? Or were they just brutal?

2

Hannibal Against Rome

A great army was marching against Rome. It had about 50,000 foot soldiers and 9,000 horse soldiers. As it marched, the army was seven miles long. Behind the soldiers were 37 big war elephants. And behind them were the many animals that carried supplies.

The leader of this army was a young general named Hannibal Barca (HAN-uh-bull BAR-cuh). Hannibal came from Carthage, a rich and powerful city-state in North Africa. Rome and Carthage had fought a long war for control of the island of Sicily (SIS-uh-lee). Finally, Carthage was forced to give up Sicily and two other islands to Rome.

Hannibal was only a boy when this happened. But his father, Hamilcar (HAM-ill-kar) Barca, the top general of Carthage, made him take an oath. Hannibal swore that some day he would get revenge against the enemy, Rome.

Carthage began to rebuild its armies in Spain, one of its colonies. It hired professional soldiers from North Africa, Spain, and islands in the Mediterranean. Hannibal became the commander of these soldiers when he was 26 years old. His men were all for him. They knew he was a great soldier, and afraid of nothing. He wore a simple officer's uniform, and often slept on the ground near them. Hannibal could count on their loyalty to the end.

Hannibal had a daring and secret plan of war against Rome. He wanted to fight the Romans on their own grounds. The Roman navy was too strong for him to risk moving his army to Italy in ships.

But there was another way for him to reach Italy. He could march his army 1,500 miles overland to get there. This meant that his army would have to cross the Alps, the highest mountains in Europe! It would be very dangerous, but Hannibal was not afraid of danger.

The long march began in May 218 B.C. From Spain, Hannibal's army moved across the south of France. One of Hannibal's first problems was to get his elephants across a wide river. Big rafts were built to ferry them across. But some of the elephants panicked on the rafts. They began to stamp and scream with fear. Some fell into the river, but they did not drown. They walked across, with only their trunks above the water.

Finally Hannibal's army reached the Alps. The mountains were covered with snow and ice. The cold and wind chilled the men to their bones. Many became sick and were left behind.

The path through the Alps was narrow, twisting, and very steep. Men and animals slipped on the ice and fell thousands of feet to their death. Often they could not see ahead of them because of snow storms. Blinded by snow, tired, and dizzy from hunger, the men stumbled on.

Then one day the men looked down and saw a warm,

green valley below them. They had made it across the Alps to Italy.

The long march had taken five months. Probably half of those who had started out had died. Those who made it were worn out. But after a long rest, they got back their strength.

The Romans were amazed when they learned that Hannibal was in Italy. They sent one army after another to capture him. Usually the Roman armies were much larger than Hannibal's. But Hannibal was such a clever general that he defeated them all. In one battle, he led the Roman army into a trap. The Romans were then surrounded and wiped out.

Hannibal could defeat Roman armies, but he could not attack the city of Rome itself. His army was not strong enough for that. So the war dragged on for 15 years. Meanwhile, Hannibal's army burned and destroyed much of the land.

Finally, the Romans found a way to get rid of Hannibal. They sent an army to North Africa to attack Carthage. This army was led by a young general, Scipio (SIP-ee-oh), who knew all of Hannibal's tricks. Carthage then called Hannibal home to defend it against Scipio. This is what Rome wanted. In 202 B.C. Scipio defeated Hannibal. Carthage had to make peace with Rome and give up Spain.

What happened to Hannibal? He ran away to the Middle East where he tried to stir up trouble for Rome. Years later, Roman agents closed in on him. Hannibal, now 65, swallowed poison and died.

What happened to Carthage? The Romans always feared that Carthage might become dangerous again. A Roman senator named Cato (KATE-oh) said over and over, "Carthage must be destroyed." Finally, in 146 B.C., a Roman army completely destroyed the city of Carthage. North Africa became a part of Rome's growing empire.

Follow the Leader

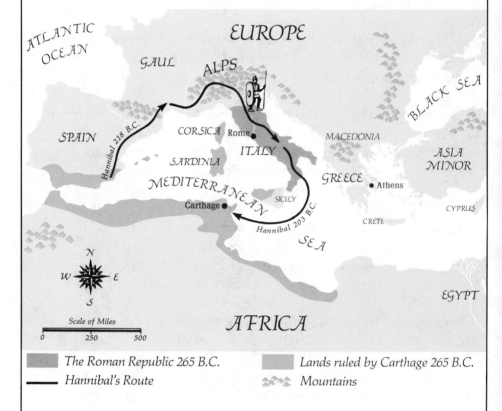

The Roman Republic 265 B.C.

—— Hannibal's Route

Lands ruled by Carthage 265 B.C.

Mountains

- In 265 B.C. Carthage controlled part of the northern coast of which continent? The southern coast of which modern-day country? Which islands?

- From which country did Hannibal and his army begin their long march to Rome? In what directions did they travel?

- What mountain range did they have to cross to get to Rome?

- When Hannibal returned to Carthage, which sea did he sail across?

- How many years went by between the time Hannibal started out for Rome and the time he left Italy to return to Carthage?

3

Conqueror
Learns from Conquered

Rome was now a great power. It had taken over all of Italy. It had defeated Carthage. It had taken control of Greece.

The Greeks were the conquered. The Romans were the conquerors. But the conquered had something to teach the conquerors. What was that?

The year: 140 B.C.

The place: a street in Rome.

The action: A rich Roman, Flavius (FLAY-vee-uhz), and his new Greek slave, Theodorus (thee-oh-DOR-uz), are taking a walk.

FLAVIUS: Theodorus, let me tell you *why* I want you to serve my family.

THEODORUS: Please do, sir.

FLAVIUS: The truth is, Theodorus, there is much I admire in you. I wish that I had gone to school like you. My father taught me all I know at home. And what was it? A little reading, writing, and arithmetic. Mainly he taught me the old Roman ways: duty to my family, loyalty to Rome, and respect for the gods. Such things are very good in their own way, Theodorus. I will not deny that. But I'll be very

honest. Compared to you Greeks, we Romans are really a little rough and crude.

THEODORUS: In certain ways I agree with you, sir. If you will pardon me for saying so, some Romans still behave a little like barbarians. The things that Romans do sometimes shock me. In my hometown in Greece, I saw Roman soldiers tear down a beautiful painting. And do you know what they did with it? They put it on the ground and played dice on it!

FLAVIUS: That's just what I mean, Theodorus. Now you Greeks are so much different. Look at all you know about art, and good books, and poetry. Look at all you know about science and politics. How much you admire wisdom, and how interested you are in *ideas!* We Romans are very good at war. We are good at building roads and bridges and stadiums. But have we ever had a man as wise as Socrates? Have we ever had a poet like Homer? Or a man who writes plays like Euripides?

THEODORUS: That is quite true, sir. But you haven't told me yet why you wanted me to serve your family.

FLAVIUS: I'm coming to that, Theodorus, I'm coming to that. You see, I want *my* children to have a *real* education. I want them to have all the things I never had. They must study music, poetry, plays, good books, and science. I want *them* to have learning, Theodorus, and not be barbarians. And my sons must learn the art of making speeches, in case they want to go into politics. These are all things that *you* can teach them, Theodorus. That's why I bought you in the first place. Do you understand?

One thing Roman conquerors learned from the Greeks they conquered was a love of drama. This Greek wall painting shows actors celebrating their success by dedicating a mask to the gods.

THEODORUS: I understand you very well, sir. But what about the old Roman ways of duty and loyalty? What about working hard and living simply? Do you want me to teach those to your children?

FLAVIUS: Oh, of course, of course, Theodorus. But let's be honest. Times are changing. My father was a simple farmer. To him, all those things were very important. "Be a good soldier, and obey your leaders," he always said. "The rest will take care of itself." And I did as I was told. But you can't expect children to believe all that stuff now, Theodorus. They've been spoiled.

When I was a boy, I lived in a house that had only one room. We all ate and slept in that one room. But later I made a lot of money in farming. Then I bought a fine house in Rome, just like one of your beautiful Greek homes.

So how can I tell *my* children to live simply? How can I tell them to work hard when they already have everything they want? What do they care about ideas such as duty and loyalty to the state? They're only interested in enjoying themselves, just like you Greeks. They like to be free, and to enjoy the good things in life. I'm afraid they will become very soft. But at least they will have learning.

Roman Values

**Be a good soldier.
Obey your leaders.
The rest will take
care of itself.**
— *Roman grandfather*

**But I want my children
to study music, poetry, plays,
good books, and science.**
— *Roman father*

**If you will pardon me
for saying so, most Romans
are still barbarians.**
— *Greek slave*

- What values does the Roman grandfather consider the most important? Is loyalty to one's country a necessary value?

- What different attitudes does the Roman father show? Why do you think his values have changed? Should they have?

- Why does the Greek slave say that most Romans are "still barbarians"? What, according to the Greek, makes a person civilized? How do you feel about his definition? Do you think the Greeks were better than the Romans?

- How do you think the Greek slave would look upon contemporary Americans—as "barbarians" or "civilized" people? What would the Roman father say?

4

Caesar: Three Views

Rome was a republic; it had no kings. But it was not very democratic. Most power was in the hands of the Senate. Its members were nobles and most of them were rich landowners.

For many years, the common people fought for a greater voice in the government. The common people won many important rights, and elected their own leaders. But wealthy Romans kept control of the Senate.

All of Rome's wars hurt its farmers badly. They were soldiers and had to leave the farms to fight. Many were ruined by the wars.

Soon, leaders of the common people began to fight with leaders of the nobles for control of the government. Bloody civil war broke out. It lasted, on and off, for more than a century.

Finally, a great Roman general named Julius Caesar (JEWL-yus SEE-zur) took power. The Senate became helpless.

Caesar was no ordinary man. To his soldiers, he was almost a god. To the common people of Rome, he was a great hero. To the Roman Senate, he was an evil man who wished to be king.

Suppose that you are in the main Roman meeting place in the year 45 B.C. Here is what some of the people are saying about Caesar:

Almost everything about Julius Caesar suggested power — even the determination written on his face.

ROMAN SOLDIER: I served with Caesar for eight years in Gaul [gawl; modern France]. I tell you there is not a greater general, or a braver man anywhere. Many times the enemy had three soldiers or more for every Roman soldier! Often we were sure the enemy would defeat us!

Once we had to fight an army of very tough Germans.

163

These Germans were hired by the Gauls to fight for them. Before the battle, we were so scared that we made out our wills. The officers begged Caesar to turn back. But Caesar reminded them of the times that Roman soldiers had smashed German armies. He said he was ready to fight with only one legion [LEE-jun; 6,000 men], if necessary. He made us feel so ashamed, we could not wait for the battle to start.

During the battle, Caesar was everywhere, shouting us on. Once he saw some men who were about to give up. He grabbed a shield and ordered them to follow him. At once, the men began to fight again behind Caesar. Finally the Germans broke and ran for their lives!

Yes, Caesar shared all our dangers. He fought with us, ate with us, and lived with us. I would fight for him again anytime, any place.

ROMAN WORKER: Julius Caesar has done more for the common people than any other Roman. Sure he is a noble and very rich. But he has always been for the poor. Look at all the things he has done for us. When he became dictator, he gave us a holiday that lasted 10 days. He spent a fortune to entertain us. There were big parades and sports events the whole time. In one stadium alone, 400 lions were killed by the gladiators [GLAD-ee-ate-orz; trained fighters]. In another, the soldiers put on a big make-believe battle. And there were plays in all the theaters.

One day Caesar gave a party for 20,000 poor people. He gave them money, bread, and oil for their lamps. He was even more generous to his soldiers. He gave each of them some land to farm.

Since then, Caesar has given jobs to army veterans and helped people who owe money. He has even allowed some very poor people to stop paying their rent. Now he is planning to build new roads, canals, temples, and theaters. Think of all the jobs that will give to the Romans who are

out of work! Yes, Julius Caesar is a great man. He is the best friend the common people ever had.

ROMAN SENATOR: Julius Caesar is the most dangerous man that Rome has ever seen. He doesn't really care about the poor people. He just buys their support by giving them shows and handing out bread. The only thing Caesar cares about is power, *power for himself.* Sure, it was the Senate which voted to make him dictator. But what could we do? Caesar had the army and the common people behind him. We were helpless. We *had* to make him dictator, or else. No one could stop him from taking power. Now he treats even the greatest senators as if they were beggars. Soon he will want to be king! Then he will get rid of the Senate, and there will be no more voting by the people. Yes, the Republic is in danger as long as Caesar lives. We must save the Republic and get rid of this evil man.

Many other senators thought the same way about Caesar. In 44 B.C., 50 of them joined in a plot to kill Caesar. One was a man Caesar had always liked, Marcus Brutus (MAR-cus BRUTE-us).

The day picked for the murder was March 15. That day, Caesar paid a visit to the Senate. One senator asked Caesar for a special favor. Caesar said, "No." Then the senator pulled back Caesar's robe, showing his neck and chest. That was the signal for murder.

Other senators rushed at Caesar with daggers and began to stab him. At first, Caesar tried to defend himself. But then he saw Brutus come at him. "You too, my friend?" he asked Brutus. Then he covered his face with his robe as Brutus stabbed him to death.

The murder of Caesar did not save the Republic. By 30 B.C., Caesar's adopted son, Octavian, took complete power in Rome. Octavian became Rome's first emperor. The Roman Republic was gone. The Roman Empire took its place.

Front Page

Your job is to arrange the headlines below in their proper order on another sheet. Put the event that happened first at the top, and so on. Then, for each headline, write a one-paragraph "news story." The story should tell what happened and why the event was important.

Roman Armies Unable To Capture Hannibal; Generals Fear Warfare Could Last for Years

RUMORS OF TREASON: JUNIUS BRUTUS' SONS PLACED UNDER ARREST

Carthage Left in Ruins; Roman Soldiers Feast To Celebrate Their Victory

CAESAR ASSASSINATED; ROMAN LEADER VICTIM OF SENATE STABBERS

Part 5

The Roman Empire

Introduction: From Greatness to Ruins

"I found Rome a city of bricks. I left it a city of marble."
This boast was made by Rome's first emperor, Octavian.
He gave Rome many beautiful buildings of marble. He made
Rome the greatest city in the ancient world. But Octavian
gave the Romans something they needed even more: peace
and good government. Octavian ruled the empire so well
that the people called him *Augustus* (aw-GUS-tus). It was a
title of great honor and respect. It meant that he was above
all other men.

With the rule of Augustus (Octavian) began 200 years of
peace and good living in the Roman Empire. During that
time, most of Rome's emperors were honest and good men.
Their laws were fair and just. Even slaves were protected
by Rome's laws. The emperors built many roads, bridges,
and harbors that helped trade.

Towns and cities grew in every part of the empire. The
farms raised enough food for all the people. The Roman

169

army kept them safe from bandits and pirates. All these things made the people of the empire loyal to Rome. Most did not mind being ruled by Rome. They did not want to be independent. Under Roman rule, they had a good life. The people of many different countries proudly called themselves *Romans*.

Rome's first emperor, Augustus (below), brought peace to his people. Page 168: Sculpture on a Roman column tells the story of the Emperor Trajan. At the base of the column, Trajan leads troops from a city wall. On second level, he makes plans for a city's defense.

Marking Time

27 B.C.	Rule of Emperor Augustus
1 A.D.	Birth of Christ
117	Rule of Hadrian
249	Rule of Decius
284	Rule of Diocletian
313	Constantine "legalizes" Christianity
330	Constantinople founded
376	Barbarians cross Danube River into Empire
395	Empire divided into East and West
410	Sack of Rome by Alaric
476	Fall of Rome (Western Empire)
1453 A.D.	Constantinople conquered by Turks

- The rule of Augustus began a period known as "the Roman Peace." If that period lasted for 200 years, in what year did it end?

- True or false? Christianity became a "legal religion" in the Roman Empire about three centuries after the birth of Christ.

- How many years after the empire was split in two did the western part fall?

- How many years after the fall of Rome did the eastern empire last?

1

The First Emperor

The year: 27 B.C.
The scene: the Roman Senate.
The action: Octavian, Caesar's adopted son, is about to make a speech.

It was all arranged in advance, very carefully. Some senators already knew what Octavian was going to say. Octavian had told them. He could count on their support. The others would surely follow their lead.

Now Octavian got up to speak. He stood near the spot where Julius Caesar had been murdered 17 years before. Some of the senators who had plotted the murder were present. But murder was not in their hearts this day. They did not care now that Octavian ruled almost as a king. His power was even greater than Caesar's. The Senate and the Roman people cared only about this:

After 100 years of bloody civil wars, Octavian had brought peace back to Rome. The Roman people were grateful to him that their lives and property were safe again. They wanted him to be their ruler, and Octavian knew it too. He too believed that Rome needed a supreme ruler to keep peace and order. But he did not want to make the same mistake as Caesar. Caesar had looked down on the Senate and made many enemies there. Octavian would be smarter.

So Octavian began his speech to the Senate. *He told the senators that he no longer wished to rule Rome.* He wanted to be just like many of the old Roman heroes. They had become dictators to save Rome in times of danger. But as soon as the danger had passed, they gave their power back to the Senate. This, Octavian said, was what he wanted to do. He was going to retire, and live as a private citizen. Rome, he said, could now become a republic again, ruled by the Senate.

Some senators knew that Octavian's speech was just a put-on. But most senators were shocked. They feared that

173

they could not rule Rome anymore. Rome had become too big for them. When Rome was a small city-state, the Senate could manage it easily. But now Rome was the head of a great empire. It ruled 100 million people of many different nations, religions, and races. The Senate had not been able to keep peace in Italy. How could it keep peace in the whole empire? A strong man with great powers was needed to rule Rome now. Octavian could not retire!

The senators began to shout that Rome *needed* a king. This was just what Octavian wanted. Caesar had made the Senate angry by taking power against its will. But now the Senate was almost begging Octavian to be king!

Octavian then agreed to stay in power. But he was a very clever man. He knew that many Romans still admired the old Republic. They would not like the idea of a king with complete power. So Octavian let the Senate rule some parts of the empire. But he kept control of the army, which meant that he was supreme. Octavian did not even call himself a king. But he used other titles that gave him all the power he needed. One of these titles was Augustus. It meant that Octavian was superhuman. He was not yet a god, but he was above all other men.

Octavian was soon called Augustus by all Romans. As Augustus, the first Roman emperor, he ruled wisely for many years. He gave to all the people of the empire just and honest government. Above all, he gave the empire peace and order. Trade and business grew, and life became better for most people. A Greek writer praised Augustus with these words:

Augustus has won for us a great peace. There are neither wars nor battles, robbers nor pirates. We may travel safely at all times from one end of the empire to the other.

While Augustus lived, many people in the empire believed he was a god. When he died in 14 A.D., the Roman Senate officially made him a god of the state.

The Emperor's Death

Suppose you are living in the Roman Empire during the rule of Octavian. The year is 14 A.D., and word of the emperor's death is spreading rapidly throughout the land. Every community is writing a message summing up the emperor's life and contributions. You have been asked to prepare a message for your town. On a separate sheet of paper, write a two- or three-paragraph description of the outstanding events in the life of Octavian. Include accomplishments which you think the emperor will be remembered for. Mention also how you and other Roman citizens felt about him as a leader. While deciding just what you'll write, here are two questions to think about: Was Octavian a truly great emperor? Or was he rather a power-hungry man who knew how to "use" people? Or was he both? Try to back your opinions with information from this chapter.

2

The Roman Peace

The scene: a busy town in Gaul.
The year: 125 A.D.
The action: Two pottery makers are having lunch.

JULIUS: Have you heard the news, Valerius [va-LAIR-ee-us]?
The Emperor Hadrian [HAY-dree-un] is planning a big
outdoor theater for our town. Think of it! Soon actors,
singers, and dancers will put on shows for us. Our town
is really getting up in the world. A few years ago, the
emperor gave us a stadium. Before that, he built our public
baths. Yes, the Romans have been good to us, Valerius.

VALERIUS: You are forgetting one important thing, Julius.
Before the Romans came, our people were free from outside
rule. We made our own rules. We did not take orders
from a Roman governor. When we were free, we stood up
like men and did things for ourselves. Now we depend on
the Romans for everything. And we imitate all their ways.
We speak *their* language, Latin, instead of our own. We use
Latin names, instead of the names of Gaul. The Romans
build temples to *their* gods, and we worship in them. No,
we are not men anymore. We have become like children.
We are well fed, but we do as we are told.

JULIUS: I am amazed to hear you talk that way, Valerius.
Roman rule is not hard at all. All we must do is pay our
taxes to Rome, and be loyal to the emperor. In return, the

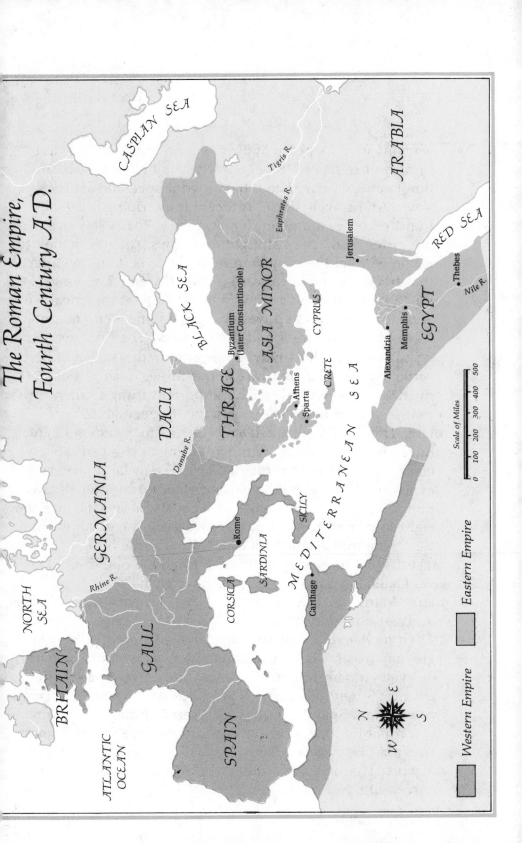

The Roman Empire, Fourth Century A.D.

ATLANTIC OCEAN

NORTH SEA

BRITAIN

GERMANIA

GAUL

SPAIN

Rhine R.

CASPIAN SEA

DACIA

Danube R.

THRACE

BLACK SEA

Byzantium (later Constantinople)

ASIA MINOR

Athens
Sparta

CRETE

CORSICA

SARDINIA

SICILY

Rome

Carthage

M E D I T E R R A N E A N   S E A

CYPRUS

Tigris R.

Euphrates R.

ARABIA

Jerusalem

RED SEA

Thebes
Nile R.

EGYPT

Alexandria

Memphis

Scale of Miles

0   100   200   300   400   500

N
W   E
S

Western Empire

Eastern Empire

Romans give us peace and protection from robbers and pirates. It is safe to travel anywhere on land or sea. You don't have to worry about being kidnapped and sold as a slave. And travel is fast. You can easily ride a horse a hundred miles a day on Roman roads. Roads connect all our cities, and are as straight as arrows. A letter mailed to Rome will get there by ship in 10 days. Is it any wonder that trade and business are so good? Aren't *we* living much better than our grandfathers? Look at this meal we are eating, with fine olives and good wine. Who taught us to plant olive trees and grape vines? The Romans!

VALERIUS: Well, Julius, maybe our grandfathers *liked* to herd cattle. And they didn't care about things such as business, or travel, or even olives. The important thing to them was that *they were independent.* Are we independent?

JULIUS: There you go again. It *might* be nice to be independent. But independence isn't worth anything unless you can enjoy it. The Romans treat us fairly. Their laws protect everyone. Why, even slaves are protected by Roman law. Suppose a slave is treated badly by his master. He has the right to protest to the Roman governor. The governor may then give him a kinder master, or even free him.

VALERIUS: All that is true, Julius. But tell me one thing. Do we Gauls have the same rights as Romans?

JULIUS: Many of us do, Valerius. Any Gaul who serves in the army or government of Rome becomes a Roman citizen. Then he has the same rights as any man born in Rome. He may become an army commander, a governor, a senator, or even emperor! That is true in almost every part of the empire. Surely you know that our great Emperor Hadrian comes from Spain! Yes, if a man serves Rome well, Rome rewards him well. I would much rather live under Roman rule than be independent.

VALERIUS: That is a pity, Julius. Unfortunately, most Gauls agree with you.

A Scale of Values

Peace, protection, and a "good life" are most important for a society. And that's what the Romans brought to Gaul. We now have a stadium, a theater, public baths, fine foods, and safety from pirates and robbers. What more could anyone want?
— *Julius*

Doing things on your own is what counts most. Even if you have to struggle, you're still your own man. Nowadays, most Gauls may be well fed, but they have to do as they are told by the Romans. They're no better than children.
— *Valerius*

How do you feel? Do you agree with Julius?

1	2	3	4	5
not at all		somewhat		completely

Do you agree with Valerius?

1	2	3	4	5
not at all		somewhat		completely

Why did you make such a choice? Thinking about the question below might help you to understand your own values:

■ Would you give up some of your independence if you could have "everything" you wanted? Or would you settle for less, knowing that you were "boss" over your own life? For example, would you prefer (a) a large allowance from your parents with your parents having a big voice in how you spend it, or (b) a part-time job which gives you less money, but allows you to spend it as you please?

3

The Young Jesus

Probably no figure in history has stirred the hearts and minds of people more than the man who was known to his followers as Jesus of Nazareth.

We know very little about Jesus' life. Jesus was not widely known during his lifetime. Outside of Galilee (GAL-uh-lee) and Judea (ju-DEE-uh), few people heard of him.

Most of what we do know about Jesus comes from four very short writings. These are known as the Gospels, and they begin the New Testament of the Bible. The Gospels do not give us many details of Jesus' life.

But the Gospels do tell us much about the things Jesus believed in. They show the great goodness of his life. This goodness convinced Jesus' followers that Jesus was no ordinary man. To them, and to Christians afterward, Jesus was blessed as the Son of God.

The followers of Jesus were at first a tiny band living near the Sea of Galilee. The movement grew and grew until it changed the course of world history. In Jesus' story people saw a life of goodness and sacrifice that expressed their own dreams and hopes.

In this chapter, we take a look at the youthful Jesus. What was Jesus like as a young person? Did he get along well with his parents? Was he playful or serious? Was he good with his studies?

Soon after the birth of Jesus, Mary and Joseph fled
with their infant son into Egypt. According to the
New Testament, they made the trip after being warned
that the Judean king wanted the child destroyed. This
wall sculpture shows the family leaving Judea on a
donkey. After the danger passed, the family returned.

These are questions we cannot really answer for sure. The Gospels tell us almost nothing about the childhood and youth of Jesus. They even leave doubt about the date of his birth. Two of the Gospels do not mention Jesus' birth at all. The Gospels of Matthew and Luke both say that Jesus was born in the town of Bethlehem. But their accounts differ.

Luke says that the Roman Emperor Augustus ordered that a population census be taken in his empire. From the town of Nazareth, Joseph and his wife, Mary, traveled to Bethlehem to sign up for the census. While they were there, Mary gave birth to her first son, Jesus. It took place in a stable, and he was laid in a manger (a feeding place for cattle). According to Luke, that was "because there was no place for them at the inn."

When was Jesus born? That date is not certain. The guesses range from 4 B.C. to 8 A.D.

Of the childhood of Jesus, we know only one incident. Luke says that Jesus' parents, who were Jewish, went each year to Jerusalem to celebrate the feast of Passover. One year, when Jesus was 12, the parents began their journey back to Nazareth. They didn't realize that Jesus had stayed behind in the city.

When they realized that Jesus was missing, they returned to Jerusalem and searched high and low for him. After three days, they found him in the great Jewish temple in Jerusalem. He was listening closely to the teachers and asking them wise questions. His mother chided him for having caused them worry. Jesus replied: "Why did you have to search for me? Did you not know that I must be about my Father's business?"

We know that Jesus grew up in Nazareth. And that is about all we know of his growing-up years. Luke does tell us that "the child grew and became strong, filled with wisdom; and the favor of God was upon him."

We can only guess that he learned the carpenter's trade,

Palestine in the Time of Jesus

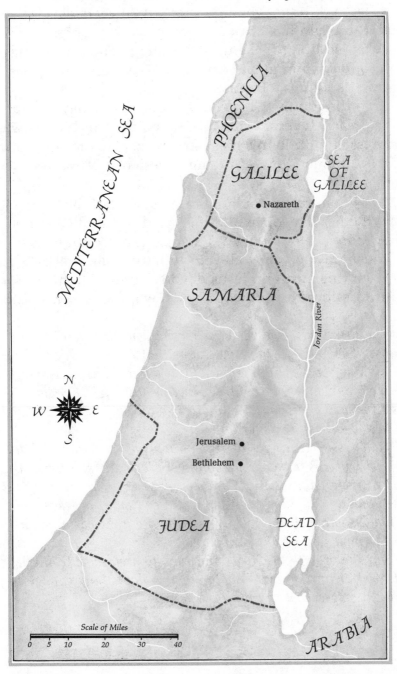

which was Joseph's trade. The Gospels do not tell us. We next learn of Jesus when he is about 30 years old. He is about to begin his work as a teacher and prophet.

What led him to take up this calling? The Gospels say he did so following his baptism by a fiery desert preacher known as John the Baptist.

According to the Gospels, Jesus went one day to hear John preach. It became the turning point of his life. He was impressed with John's message. He decided to be baptized. It was a tremendously moving experience. Mark describes it this way:

"At the moment when he came up out of the water, Jesus saw the heavens open and the Spirit of God like a dove, descending upon him. And a voice spoke from heaven: 'Thou art my Son, my Beloved; with thee I am well pleased.'"

From this moment, Jesus devoted himself to his mission. This mission was to preach God's word for saving mankind.

The task that Jesus began when he was about 30 led to the Cross. The New Testament tells us that Jesus reappeared to his disciples after the Crucifixion. This is known as the Resurrection. After reappearing, Jesus is believed to have told his disciples to "go forth to every part of the world, and proclaim the Good News to the whole creation."

His message became the foundation for the new religion, Christianity. A few of Jesus' followers dedicated the rest of their lives to spreading the Christian faith. They wandered through the lands around the Mediterranean Sea, telling of Jesus' teaching. Soon Christianity had followers throughout the eastern end of the Roman Empire. Even in Rome itself.

But the growth of Christianity led to a clash with the leaders of the Roman Empire. This brought a bloody and savage period, which is described in the next chapter.

The Good Samaritan

Jesus often used parables (stories) to teach important ideas. Read the parable below. It is adapted from the Gospel of St. Luke. Then answer the questions which follow.

. . . There was a man on his way to Jericho, when robbers attacked him and beat him up, leaving him half dead. It so happened that a citizen was going down that road; when he saw the man he walked on by, on the other side. In the same way a second citizen also came there, went over and looked at the man, and then walked on by, on the other side. But a certain Samaritan (a man from the district of Samaria) who was traveling that way came upon him, and when he saw the man his heart was filled with pity. He went over to him, poured oil and wine on his wounds, and bandaged them. Then he put the man on his own animal, and took him to an inn where he took care of him. . . .

Then Jesus asked his student: Which one of the three passersby acted in the right way?

■ What would your answer be to Jesus' question?

■ What is the message of this parable? Does it still have meaning today?

■ What is meant by the term "good Samaritan"?

■ Do you think most people today would do what the good Samaritan did? If you can, give specific examples to back up your answer.

4

A Challenge
to the Emperors

*Not all people in the empire were well treated. Christians
were treated badly at times. Why? Christians would not worship
Rome's emperors as gods. Many of them would not serve in the
Roman army or government. Some emperors tried to force
Christians to give up their beliefs. Many Christians who refused
were put in jail, or even killed.*

The year: 250 A.D.

The scene: the home of Marcellus (mar-SELL-us), a Roman
merchant.

The action: Marcellus and his friend, Titus (TIE-tus), are
having dinner.

TITUS: Well, Marcellus, it looks like the Emperor Decius [DEE-
shuss] is cracking down on the Christians. He says that
they must swear loyalty to the gods of Rome. If they do,
they will be all right. But if they refuse, they will be put
in jail. They will get no food or water until they change
their minds. What do you think of that?

MARCELLUS: I'm all for it, Titus. I say it's about time we stopped babying those Christians. Our courts have been much too easy on them. Most of our judges actually seem to protect them. What happens when a man is accused of being a Christian? First, the judge demands all kinds of proof that it is true. Well, it's hard to prove that a person is a Christian, Titus. You know that. Those people are very clever. They have their meetings in secret, usually at night.

So what does the judge do? He throws the case out of court. Or he finds some other excuse to let the person off easy. The person is sent to work in the mines or goes to jail. Six months later, he or she is pardoned, and then is back on the streets again.

I tell you, Titus, we have to get tough with those people. I say we should put them all in jail and throw away the key. Or better yet, throw them to the lions. That's what some of our governors do at times. It's really the best way.

TITUS: Tell me, Marcellus, why are you so bitter about these Christians? I have a number of Christian friends, and they are really very good people. In many ways, they behave much better than the average Roman. Most Romans today seem to care only about pleasure. They want to be amused constantly by festivals and games. But these Christians are different. They don't care much about money, and they are content to live simply. They are good family people— they don't drink or carry on at night. Above all, they want so much to do good. They try to outdo each other with kindness and patience and modesty. Surely, Marcellus, such people do not deserve the kind of treatment you're suggesting.

MARCELLUS: Titus, you amaze me. I never thought I would hear a friend of mine defend Christians! Don't you understand, Titus, that these people are enemies of the state? They believe in only One God, and refuse to worship our Roman gods. They refuse to admit that our Roman emperors are gods. They predict that the Roman Empire will come to an end. They say that the Kingdom of Heaven will take its place! Many refuse to serve in the army or the government. What would become of our empire if every man refused to become a soldier? Right now, Marcellus, the German barbarians are attacking our borders. The empire is in great danger. And any man who will not fight for it is a traitor!

TITUS: The empire must be defended, of course. But let's be honest, Marcellus. How many Romans serve in the army these days? More and more we are hiring soldiers from outside Italy to fight for us. Besides, how many Christians are there? Maybe one person out of 20 in our empire is a Christian. There just aren't enough Christians to help us much in our defense.

MARCELLUS: True, but the number of Christians keeps growing. They are such stubborn people. They never stop preaching about their Lord, Jesus Christ. They say that they must be loyal to him, rather than our emperors. And who was this Jesus Christ? I hear that he was a poor Jewish carpenter in Galilee. How can they call a beggar like that the Son of God?

TITUS: I'm sure I don't know, Marcellus. But in our empire people worship many different gods. And we Romans have usually permitted them to worship as they please. Should we not also permit the Christians to worship their God and the man they consider His Son?

MARCELLUS: Do not compare the Christians with other people in our empire! Other people have their own gods, it is true. But they also respect our emperor as a god, and other Roman gods. The Christians say that all our gods are really evil spirits! For this they must be severely punished.

Two Letters

Dear Cousin,
You've asked me about the Christians. I hope this letter will answer most of your questions.

Actually, I think all Christians are enemies of Rome. Why, they believe in only One God and refuse to pray to our gods. They even say the emperor isn't a god.

As you know, Germans are attacking our borders. But Christians won't fight for us because of their beliefs. What do you think of people who refuse to help their country in time of danger? I call them traitors.

If you ask me, all Christians should be thrown into jail. Or better yet, thrown to the lions.
— Marcellus

Dear Cousin,
You've asked me about the Christians. I hope this letter will answer most of your questions.

Actually, I have many Christian friends. And it's true they pray to only One God. But all citizens worship as they please in Rome. Why treat Christians differently?

Yes, it's also true that Christians don't serve in the army. But most Romans don't either. We mostly use hired soldiers to fight for Rome now.

Frankly, I think most Christians act better than Romans. Christians always try to help others. Why, just yesterday a Christian helped me fix the wheel of my chariot.
— Titus

These letters have been sent by Marcellus and Titus to cousins who live in far ends of the Roman Empire. Why has each writer reached a different opinion? If Roman leaders let other people worship as they pleased, why did they persecute Christians? Do you think many people are afraid of groups which differ from the majority? If you had been alive during the existence of the Roman Empire, how would you have felt about the Christians?

5

The Enemy Outside

After about 200 years of power, the Roman Empire began to weaken. There were many reasons for the decline (see page 199). One important reason was that tribesmen from Germany and other areas began to attack the empire. What were these warriors like? This chapter gives you some important clues.

The German warriors were having a party. They had hunted and killed some wild animals in the forest. Then they roasted them over big fires. Now they were eating so much that they felt stuffed. They were big, strong men. They wore woolen trousers and cloaks made of fur. They had powerful muscles.

Suddenly a group of strangers appeared. They were also warriors, but they came from another village. They seemed friendly and were invited to join the party. Then the warriors of both villages began to brag about their chiefs. (The chief of a German village was usually the bravest and strongest warrior.) The bragging led to an argument. Each side swore

As the Roman Empire weakened, its most serious threat
came from the north. Roman soldiers often dealt with
barbarian prisoners by cutting off their heads. This
wall sculpture shows some of the grizzly details.

that its chief was a better soldier than the other. Finally, a bloody fight started. Two or three men were killed before the strangers ran away.

The next day, the village chief called his warriors to a meeting. The warriors came with their spears and shields. Then the chief began to speak. He said that the strangers had insulted the honor of their village. The strangers were invited to share their food and drink. But they had started a fight, and men were killed. The chief asked the warriors: Would they stand for such an insult? Or would they fight for the honor of their chief and their village?

The warriors gave their answer. They began to bang their spears and shields together. Then they shouted, "We'll fight!" Now the warriors were happy. There was nothing they liked more than fighting.

The land of Germany was filled with rough warriors like these. The people of Rome called the Germans "barbarians." The Germans did not live in cities with houses of stone. They lived in forests, and their homes were houses made of logs. They raised only a little food by farming. They got their food mainly by keeping cattle and by hunting. They moved around much of the time, and carried all their goods in wagons. They had no writing, and little skill in the arts. They used very little metal. Pots and pans made of clay were all they had.

The Romans looked down on the German barbarians, but they also feared them. They worried about the warriors breaking into their empire. For a long time, the Romans were able to keep the warriors out. But later the Roman Empire and its army became weak. Romans no longer served in the army. The emperors had to hire outsiders to defend their borders. Finally, they even had to hire Germans to fight other Germans! At last Rome could not keep the warriors out any longer. Many of them overran large sections of the empire and settled down. The Romans could not stop them.

action project

Puzzling It Out

Get ready to solve another word puzzle. First, copy the diagram onto a separate sheet of paper. If you need to review the directions, turn back to page 135. Remember the boxes in the top part, when filled in, will contain a question. The answer to that question is in the white circles which run down the bottom part of the puzzle.

1	2	3	4	5

6	7	8	9	10	11

12	13	14

15	16	17

18	19	20	21

22	23	24	25	26	27	28

?

A. To melt, rhymes with raw.

B. The upper part of the leg.

C. Dogs sometimes do this; means the same as plead.

D. Sailors aboard a ship; rhymes with true.

E. A female pronoun (ends with a vowel).

F. I am, you are, he _____ .

G. This number multiplied by itself equals 100.

H. Cattle and pigs may live here; rhymes with alarm.

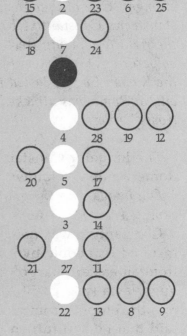

6

City of Constantine

*Some Roman emperors tried very hard to make the empire
stronger. One of them was the Emperor Constantine (CON-
stan-teen). Constantine became a Christian and gave Christians
the right to worship freely. Constantine was an important
emperor in other ways. Because of a decision he made, part of
the Roman Empire lasted for almost a thousand years after the
city of Rome was attacked and captured by warlike tribesmen
from Germany.*

The Emperor Constantine was in trouble. The people of
Rome wanted to know:
*Did he worship the gods of Rome as a Roman emperor was
expected to do?*
Constantine was not liked in the city of Rome. He had
insulted its people by not living there. Constantine came
from an eastern part of the empire. Today it is called
Yugoslavia (you-go-SLAH-vee-uh). Constantine chose to
rule the empire from cities in the east. The people of Rome
said that he had turned his back on them.

Constantine had made the Romans angry in other ways. Most of them still believed in the old Roman gods. These Romans were pagans (PAY-guns). But Constantine said that he had become a Christian. He had given Christians the right to worship freely. Now he was giving money to build great churches in Rome. He had even chosen a Christian governor for the city. The Roman Senate and the people did not like it at all.

Now, in 326 A.D., Constantine was visiting Rome. He had come back to celebrate an important event. It was 20 years since he had become emperor. On this day, the soldiers were lined up for a parade. They were going to march, with their emperor, to the great temple of Jupiter (JOO-puh-ter). Jupiter was the chief god of Rome. But Constantine refused to march in the parade. He would not bow down to a pagan god!

The people and the senators began to curse Constantine. A riot almost broke out, but the soldiers kept order. They were still loyal to their emperor.

Constantine had never liked Rome. Now he liked it even less. He began to think about building a new capital city for the empire. He wanted this city to be in the east, close to Asia Minor (modern Turkey). What were his reasons?

• The towns and farms of the east were rich. The east had not suffered as much damage as had the west from the attacks of the German tribes.

• The best soldiers in the empire now came from the east. Some of these soldiers, like Constantine, had become Roman emperors. A city in the east would be good for the defense of the empire.

• The east had many more Christians than the west. Christianity had started in the eastern part of the empire. Constantine knew that the Christians would support him.

Constantine finally chose an old Greek city called Byzantium (buh-ZAN-she-um). Only a very narrow piece of water separated it from Asia Minor. Constantine began to

Once he became emperor, Constantine gave greater power to the Church. He made Christianity legal and finally took up the faith himself. In this painting he is shown leading a Christian Pope into Rome.

rebuild the city. Workers came from all over the empire to do the job. Constantine wanted his new capital to be as great as Rome. And he did not care how much it cost. New taxes would take care of that.

The new capital soon began to look much like Rome. The Great Palace of Constantine was built next to a big racetrack. Constantine could watch the races from his palace windows. The forum, or meeting place, was paved with marble. A golden statue of Constantine stood on a high column in the center. The sidewalks of the main avenue were decorated with hundreds of bronze statues. Most of them were stolen by Constantine's agents from cities in Greece. The public baths were in a big building with walls of marble. Constantine also built a fine church.

Constantine named his new capital after himself. He called it Constantinople (con-stan-tuh-NO-pel) — the city of Constantine. The city was ready on May 11, 330. There were parades, feasts, and games for the next 40 days. Both Christian and pagan priests prayed for Constantine. To many people, he was a god.

At the racetrack, soldiers had a parade in his honor. They wore their best uniforms and held white candles in their hands. Some guarded a golden statue of Constantine that was carried in a wagon. The people bowed down to the statue and praised the emperor. When the statue came to Constantine, he saluted it. Then he ordered the same parade to be held on each birthday of the city.

What made Constantinople so important? After Constantine died, the Roman Empire split in two. The western half was ruled by one emperor in Rome. The eastern half was ruled by another emperor in Constantinople. Tribesmen soon overran and destroyed the western empire (see next chapter). But the eastern empire held off the tribesmen. It lasted more than a thousand years. The laws, arts, and sciences of Rome and Greece lived on in the eastern Roman Empire.

Roving Reporter

Imagine that you are a roving reporter in the ancient Roman Empire. You interview various citizens about their feelings toward the Emperor Constantine. Then you interview the emperor himself. On a separate sheet of paper, write down the responses you think each of your "subjects" would give.

You would ask: **He/she would answer:**

1 A ROMAN SENATOR

Do you think Constantine
has treated Rome fairly?

2 A CHRISTIAN WOMAN

Do you think Constantine
is a friend to the Christians?

3 A CITIZEN OF
CONSTANTINOPLE

Why do many people here
consider Constantine a god?

4 EMPEROR CONSTANTINE

Why did you decide to build
your new city in the East?

Is the new city like Rome
in any ways?

7

The Fall of Rome

The people of Rome were in a panic. A large army of German tribesmen had crossed the Alps and entered Italy. These tribesmen, called Goths, spread terror in the northern cities. They killed people without pity, and stole everything they could carry away. Now, in 410 A.D., they were marching on Rome. And the city was helpless. It had no power at all to stop the Goths.

Rome had changed very much since its early days. Its senators had become soft with easy living. Many lived in great palaces with slaves and servants to wait on them. They wasted their money on big parties that lasted for days. They ate from gold or silver dishes, and wore robes of silk. They rode around in fancy carriages followed by their slaves. These senators would not even *think* of going to war.

What about the common people of Rome? The tough farmers had lost their lands a long time ago. Rome was now filled with many thousands of men who had no jobs. Many were freed slaves or drifters from all over the empire. They lived in dark and crowded slums. But they were given free

bread, cooking oil, and cheap wine every month. The emperors also gave them free entertainment on many days. They watched slaves attack and kill wild animals in big stadiums. Or they cheered their favorite drivers in dangerous chariot races. These drifters had also become soft. They were no use at all as soldiers.

Where was the young Emperor Honorius (huh-NOR-ee-us) while the Goths were marching on Rome? He was in a safe place a long way from the city. He did not even try to help Rome. He was afraid of the Goths.

The Goths were soon outside the walls of Rome. They surrounded the city and did not let any food in. Soon the Romans were starving. They ate anything they could find— even rats. Thousands of people died of hunger, and there was no place to bury them. Then disease spread all over the city, and many more people died.

Finally, slaves who hated the Romans opened one of the city gates. It was midnight. The Goths, led by their chief, Alaric (AL-uh-rik), charged in. They broke into homes and stole all the jewels, gold, and silver they found. They killed thousands of men, women, and children. Many slaves took revenge on their Roman masters and murdered them. The streets of Rome were soon filled with dead bodies. The Goths set fire to part of the city, and many buildings burned down. Thousands of Romans were taken as slaves. For five days Rome was a city of terror and sadness.

The Goths left Rome on the sixth day. Their wagons were piled high with stolen goods. They went south to rob the cities there. But Alaric soon died, and then the Goths left Italy. Rome tried to rebuild itself and hold its empire. But it was hopeless. Other groups of tribesmen soon overran almost every part of the western empire. In 476 A.D. they drove out the last Roman emperor. Tribal kings and chiefs now ruled all of Western Europe. The Roman Empire in the West was dead.

Front Page

Your job is to arrange the headlines below in proper order on another sheet. Put the event that happened first at the top, and so on. Then, for each headline, write a one-paragraph "news story." It should tell what happened and why the event was important.

**WESTERN EMPIRE FALLS;
HEAVY LOSSES REPORTED
AS GOTHS LOOT ROME**

**Latest Poll Results Show
Satisfaction in Empire;
Gauls Especially Happy
Living Under Roman Rule**

**Germans Threaten Empire;
Rome Steps Up Patrols To
Tighten Border Security**

**Constantinople Hailed
As "Rome of the East";
New City Will Be Safe
From Invaders' Attack**

**ROMAN SENATE NAMES
OCTAVIAN AS EMPEROR;
NEW LEADER PLEDGES
BETTER TIMES AHEAD**

Index

MAPS: